PATHWAYS CHARTER SCHOOL
CAIS Program
620 Hoen Avenue
Santa Rosa CA 95405

Other Kaplan Books for California Students:

Parent's Guide to the California STAR Program: Grades 3–4

California STAR Program Workbook: Grade 3

California STAR Program Workbook: Grade 9

California STAR* Program Workbook

Grade 8

* Standardized Testing and Reporting

By the Staff of Kaplan, Inc.

Simon & Schuster

New York · London · Singapore · Sydney · Toronto

† The California STAR Program is a product of the California Department of Education, which is not affiliated with this book.

Kaplan Publishing

Published by Simon & Schuster
1230 Avenue of the Americas
New York, NY 10020

For bulk sales to schools, colleges, and universities, please contact: Order Department, Simon & Schuster, 100 Front Street, Riverside, NJ 08075. Phone: 1-800-223-2336, Fax: 1-800-943-9831.

The material in this book is up-to-date at the time of publication. The California Department of Education may have instituted changes after this book was published. Please read all materials you receive regarding the California STAR Program carefully.

Project Editor: Larissa Shmailo
Contributing Editors: Marc Bernstein, Marcy Bullmaster, Phillip Vlahakis
Page Layout: Jobim Rose
Art and Design: Denise Hoff, Alisa Caratozzolo, Sarah Carnevale, Kevin Rafter, Jobim Rose
Cover Design: Cheung Tai
Production Editor: Maude Spekes
Managing Editor: Dave Chipps
Executive Editor: Del Franz

Manufactured in the United States of America

Published Simultaneously in Canada

Special thanks: Drew Johnson, Rudy Robles

December 2000

10 9 8 7 6 5 4 3 2 1

ISBN 0-7432-0488-3

CONTENTS

All of the practice questions in this book were created by the authors to illustrate question types. They are not actual test questions. For more information on the STAR program, including sample questions and answers and past STAR test results, visit the California Department of Education's Web site at www.cde.ca.gov.

Introduction to the STAR

This workbook will help you prepare for the California Grade 8 STAR tests. The two exams in this book will help you test your knowledge of important concepts in math and English. These exams will also give you a feel for answering multiple-choice questions and taking tests under timed conditions. These are not "sample" STAR tests. But the exams in this workbook will give you a chance to learn test-taking skills and find out what you know and what you don't know. That way, you can pay special attention to your weakest areas and be prepared to do well on the day of the real STAR test.

What Is the STAR Program?

The STAR is the California Department of Education's Standardized Testing and Reporting (STAR) Program. The STAR test for grade 8 consists of multiple-choice tests in Mathematics—Problem Solving; Mathematics—Procedures; Reading Vocabulary; Reading Comprehension; Language; and Spelling. There are also two additional multiple-choice tests in Language Arts and Mathematics that are designed to determine how well students have learned the content of the state's curriculum. STAR administration varies by school district, but the state recommends that no more than two subtests be given on one day.

Is the STAR Test Important?

Performance on the STAR test has a large impact on both the student and the school district. Based on test performance, the state ranks all schools, showing how well or how poorly their students fared on the exam. Schools that do badly may face the possibility of having superintendents, principals, or teachers fired based on their low performance, although for now there is no specific plan in place to deal with low-scoring schools. As for the individual eighth-grader, it is up to each school district to decide whether students who fail the STAR tests can be promoted to the next grade. The STAR tests are not necessarily the sole factor, however. Other factors, such as attendance, teacher recommendation, and performance on local assessment tests may also be used by the local district to decide whether or not a student can advance to the next grade level.

How to Use This Book

This book contains two tests. Each covers subjects such as reading, math, language, and spelling. Start by taking Practice Test A. There is no need to study or prepare for this exam since the goal is to discover how well you can score without any preparation.

Of course, time yourself when taking the test, and limit yourself to the time listed and the start of each test section. You don't have to complete all the sections in a row, but do not stop working on any one section until your time is up. Taking breaks during a section is not the best way to prepare for the STAR. There will be no breaks during the real STAR.

The tests you'll be taking are divided into the following sections:

Subject	Number of Questions	Time
Reading Vocabulary	30 questions	20 minutes
Reading Comprehension	54 questions	50 minutes
Mathematics—Problem Solving	52 questions	50 minutes
Mathematics—Procedures	30 questions	30 minutes
Language	48 questions	45 minutes
Spelling	30 questions	25 minutes

Remember that there is no guessing penalty on the STAR test—that means no points are subtracted for wrong answers. So answer all the questions even if you have to guess. Use process of elimination—crossing out the answers you know are wrong—to help you make better guesses.

It's also a good idea to write down all your work, especially for the math questions. Try to work at a steady pace, and don't get stuck on any one question. If you have time, you can always go back to look at it again.

Once you finish the first test, look at the **Answers and Explanations** section that follows Practice Test A. Your answers to the questions on the first test—and specifically, the ones you answered incorrectly—will guide you to the subjects you need to focus on. If you scored low in one area, call that a "Hot Spot." You should find extra help for that subject. Ask your teachers, parents, or friends for advice.

While working on your Hot Spots, take some time to look over the **Strategy Recap** section of this book. This is a summary of the some of the information found in the **Answers and Explanations** section. You may have already used some of these strategies on your own during the first test, but it's important you try to use them all on the second exam. Approaching a question with the proper strategy not only improves your chances of getting that question right, it also helps reduce your anxiety about the test. By learning all the strategies, you should gain a better understanding of what needs to be done to score well on the STAR, and having that knowledge should increase your confidence. So on the the first test, you'll answer questions without a predetermined plan, but after studying the **Strategy Recap** section, you can approach the next test with a clearer idea of how to answer each particular question type.

Once you have worked on your Hot Spots and studied the various strategies, take the second exam. Make sure you take each section under timed conditions. Your score on the second test should be higher than your score on the first test because:

(1) You have studied more.

(2) You are comfortable with the look and feel of the test.

After you take and grade your second exam, look for areas in which your score was low. Keep focusing your study time on those areas.

If your score on the second test falls or stays the same, don't worry. Remember, this is just practice and these tests don't count! A low score just means you have more work to do. Sometimes scores drop because you are trying out a new test-taking technique for the first time. You are doing the right thing by testing yourself and studying. Keep practicing and you will be ready for the STAR on test day.

For more information about the STAR Program, and to view sample questions and past STAR results, visit the California Department of Education's Web site at www.cde.ca.gov.

Managing Test Stress

The countdown has begun. Your date with the test is looming on the horizon. Anxiety is on the rise. The butterflies in your stomach have gone ballistic and your thinking is getting cloudy. Maybe you think you won't be ready. Maybe you already know your stuff, but you're going into panic mode anyway. Don't panic! It's possible to tame that anxiety and stress—*before* and *during* the test.

Remember, some stress is normal and good. Anxiety is a motivation to study. The adrenaline that gets pumped into your bloodstream when you're stressed helps you stay alert and think more clearly. But if you feel that the tension is so great that it's preventing you from using your study time effectively, here are some things you can do to get it under control.

Take Control

Lack of control is a prime cause of stress. Research shows that if you don't have a sense of control over what's happening in your life, you can easily end up feeling helpless and hopeless. Try to identify the sources of the stress you feel. Which ones of these can you do something about? Can you find ways to reduce the stress you're feeling about any of these sources?

Focus on Your Strengths

Make a list of areas of strength you have that will help you do well on the test. We all have strengths, and recognizing your own is like having reserves of solid gold at Fort Knox. You'll be able to draw on your reserves as you need them, helping you solve difficult questions, maintain confidence, and keep test stress and anxiety at a distance. And every time you recognize a new area of strength, solve a challenging problem, or score well on a practice test, you'll increase your reserves.

Imagine Yourself Succeeding

Close your eyes and imagine yourself in a relaxing situation. Breathe easily and naturally. Now, think of a real-life situation in which you scored well on a test or did well on an assignment. Focus on this success. Now turn your thoughts to the STAR, and keep your thoughts and feelings in line with that successful experience. Don't make comparisons between them; just imagine yourself taking the upcoming test with the same feelings of confidence and relaxed control.

Set Realistic Goals

Facing your problem areas gives you some distinct advantages. What do you want to accomplish in the time remaining? Make a list of realistic goals. You can't help feeling more confident when you know you're actively improving your chances of earning a higher test score.

Exercise Your Frustrations Away

Whether it's jogging, biking, pushups, or a pickup basketball game, physical exercise will stimulate your mind and body, and improve your ability to think and concentrate. A surprising number of students fall out of the habit of regular exercise, ironically because they're spending so much time prepping for exams. A little physical exertion will help to keep your mind and body in sync and sleep better at night.

Avoid Drugs

Using drugs (prescription or recreational) specifically to prepare for and take a big test is definitely self-defeating. (And if they're illegal drugs, you may end up with a bigger problem than the STAR on your hands.) Mild stimulants, such as coffee or cola can sometimes help as you study, since they keep you alert. On the down side, too much of these can also lead to agitation, restlessness, and insomnia. It all depends on your tolerance for caffeine.

Eat Well

Good nutrition will help you focus and think clearly. Eat plenty of fruits and vegetables, low-fat protein such as fish, skinless poultry, beans, and legumes, and whole grains such as brown rice, whole wheat bread, and pastas. Don't eat a lot of sugar and high-fat snacks, or salty foods.

Keep Breathing

Conscious attention to breathing is an excellent way to manage stress while you're taking the test. Most of the people who get into trouble during tests take shallow breaths: They breathe using only their upper chests and shoulder muscles, and may even hold their breath for long periods of time. Conversely, those test takers who breathe deeply in a slow, relaxed manner are likely to be in better control during the session.

Stretch

If you find yourself getting spaced out or burned out as you're studying or taking the test, stop for a brief moment and stretch. Even though you'll be pausing for a moment, it's a moment well spent. Stretching will help to refresh you and refocus your thoughts.

Practice Test A

Section 1:
Reading Vocabulary

20 Minutes

30 Questions

Directions: *Make sure you have a watch to time yourself and a No. 2 pencil. When you are ready, start timing yourself, and spend 20 minutes answering the questions in this section. Mark your answers on the answer sheet provided. If you are finished before the time is up, check over your work.*

Reading Vocabulary

Synonyms

Directions

Select the word or set of words that mean the same as the underlined word.

Sample

To <u>congratulate</u> means to —

- Ⓐ discuss
- ● praise
- Ⓒ laugh
- Ⓓ listen

1 To <u>contract</u> means to —

- Ⓐ lengthen
- Ⓑ lecture
- Ⓒ squeeze
- Ⓓ detract

2 To <u>depress</u> is to —

- Ⓕ push down
- Ⓖ lift up
- Ⓗ lighten
- Ⓙ renew

3 <u>Grave</u> means —

- Ⓐ easy
- Ⓑ serious
- Ⓒ happy
- Ⓓ simple

4 To <u>converse</u> means to —

- Ⓕ exchange
- Ⓖ reverse
- Ⓗ destroy
- Ⓙ discuss

5 A <u>calamity</u> is a kind of —

- Ⓐ disaster
- Ⓑ comedy
- Ⓒ estimate
- Ⓓ village

6 To <u>declare</u> something means to —

- Ⓕ allow it
- Ⓖ criticize it
- Ⓗ announce it
- Ⓙ hear it

7 <u>Doubt</u> is —

- Ⓐ greed
- Ⓑ anger
- Ⓒ distrust
- Ⓓ ignorance

8 <u>Mainly</u> means —

- Ⓕ chiefly
- Ⓖ truly
- Ⓗ fortunately
- Ⓙ visibly

GO ON

9 __Strict__ means —

- (A) unhappy
- (B) severe
- (C) cautious
- (D) silent

10 Someone who is __observant__ is —

- (F) frightened
- (G) dependable
- (H) attentive
- (J) relaxed

11 To __tutor__ is to —

- (A) teach
- (B) taunt
- (C) pay
- (D) bore

12 __Cancer__ is a kind of —

- (F) wound
- (G) injury
- (H) disease
- (J) accident

13 __Luxurious__ means —

- (A) small
- (B) necessary
- (C) fancy
- (D) flushed

14 Someone who is __courteous__ is —

- (F) short
- (G) polite
- (H) careful
- (J) violent

15 __Cryptic__ means —

- (A) passive
- (B) enraged
- (C) puzzling
- (D) enthusiastic

16 To __vilify__ means to—

- (F) praise
- (G) admire
- (H) criticize
- (J) analyze

GO ON

Multiple Meanings

Directions

Read through the sentence in the box. Then select the answer in which the underlined word has the same meaning as the underlined word in the boxed sentence.

Sample

> **The group sounded best in a live concert.**

In which sentence does the word live mean the same thing as in the sentence above?

- Ⓐ The Johnsons live on Beal Street.
- Ⓑ The building repair exposed several live wires.
- ⬤ The TV network promised a live broadcast.
- Ⓓ The refugees live in hope of change.

17

> **He swam faster with the current.**

In which sentence does the word current mean the same thing as in the sentence above?

- Ⓐ My current driver's license expires soon.
- Ⓑ The test questions covered current events.
- Ⓒ The air current lifted the plane.
- Ⓓ The current fashion is for long dresses.

18

> **Since we were hungry, we ordered a medium pizza.**

In which sentence does the word medium mean the same thing as in the sentence above?

- Ⓕ Television is a medium of global communication.
- Ⓖ Her interest in the occult led her to consult a medium.
- Ⓗ Despite his recent growth spurt, he wore a medium tee shirt.
- Ⓙ I like my hamburgers well done, but my steak medium.

19

> **They store their canned goods in the basement.**

In which sentence does the word store mean the same thing as in the sentence above?

- Ⓐ Most farmers store grain in their silos.
- Ⓑ The store went out of business, a victim of the recession.
- Ⓒ The battle had depleted our store of ammunition.
- Ⓓ The chef's store of provisions included many delicacies.

GO ON

20 I could hardly <u>bear</u> to watch the end of the movie.

In which sentence does the word <u>bear</u> mean the same thing as in the sentence above?

- (F) When I was sick, I couldn't <u>bear</u> solid food.
- (G) We tied all our food in a tree so a <u>bear</u> couldn't get to it.
- (H) <u>Bear</u> in mind that this is a very important decision.
- (J) This assignment was a real <u>bear</u>!

21 In the library, you must <u>conduct</u> yourself properly.

In which sentence does the word <u>conduct</u> mean the same thing as in the sentence above?

- (A) Cadets have to <u>conduct</u> themselves according to the rules.
- (B) It is thrilling to <u>conduct</u> an entire orchestra.
- (C) Rubber does not <u>conduct</u> electricity well.
- (D) The prisoner got time off for good <u>conduct</u>.

22 The ship's radar was able to <u>spot</u> the iceberg.

In which sentence does the word <u>spot</u> mean the same thing as in the sentence above?

- (F) The advertiser purchased a radio <u>spot</u> for his commercial.
- (G) She couldn't wear the dress because it had a <u>spot</u> on it.
- (H) I couldn't <u>spot</u> him in the crowd.
- (J) Her coach offered to <u>spot</u> the gymnast as she practiced.

23 I had to appear at the <u>court</u> last October.

In which sentence does the word <u>court</u> mean the same thing as in the sentence above?

- (A) If you play by the railroad tracks, you will <u>court</u> danger.
- (B) An attorney will be appointed to you by the <u>court</u>.
- (C) We had to run sprints up and down the basketball <u>court</u>.
- (D) The lad will <u>court</u> the fair maiden.

GO ON

Vocabulary-in-Context

Directions

In the sentence below, use the words surrounding the underlined word to figure out what it means.

Sample

Jeff reached the <u>summit</u> of the mountain, then began a long descent. <u>Summit</u> means —

- (A) valley
- ● top
- (C) clouds
- (D) ridge

24 Although the movie had been confusing, its <u>conclusion</u> finally answered all my questions. <u>Conclusion</u> means —

- (F) review
- (G) ending
- (H) beginning
- (J) protagonist

25 When I read the directions, I learned that the <u>function</u> of the button was to make the tape go backwards. <u>Function</u> means—

- (A) description
- (B) opposite
- (C) goal
- (D) purpose

26 Kara gives <u>unique</u> birthday gifts because she always comes up with things no one else would think of. <u>Unique</u> means —

- (F) expensive
- (G) handmade
- (H) distinctive
- (J) artistic

27 Though I was the one who came up with the <u>concept</u> for the design, she came up with the final product. <u>Concept</u> means —

- (A) color
- (B) idea
- (C) money
- (D) sketch

28 Because my stomach hurt, I ate only a small <u>portion</u> of my meal. <u>Portion</u> means —

- (F) partition
- (G) majority
- (H) potion
- (J) part

29 Since I had lost a few checker pieces, I used pennies to <u>represent</u> the missing ones. <u>Represent</u> means to —

- (A) replace
- (B) reject
- (C) support
- (D) revise

30 Since no one thought the team would do well, the fans were <u>ecstatic</u> when they won! <u>Ecstatic</u> means —

- (F) disappointed
- (G) angry
- (H) happy
- (J) mysterious

STOP

Answer Sheet

1 (A) (B) (C) (D)

2 (F) (G) (H) (J)

3 (A) (B) (C) (D)

4 (F) (G) (H) (J)

5 (A) (B) (C) (D)

6 (F) (G) (H) (J)

7 (A) (B) (C) (D)

8 (F) (G) (H) (J)

9 (A) (B) (C) (D)

10 (F) (G) (H) (J)

11 (A) (B) (C) (D)

12 (F) (G) (H) (J)

13 (A) (B) (C) (D)

14 (F) (G) (H) (J)

15 (A) (B) (C) (D)

16 (F) (G) (H) (J)

17 (A) (B) (C) (D)

18 (F) (G) (H) (J)

19 (A) (B) (C) (D)

20 (F) (G) (H) (J)

21 (A) (B) (C) (D)

22 (F) (G) (H) (J)

23 (A) (B) (C) (D)

24 (F) (G) (H) (J)

25 (A) (B) (C) (D)

26 (F) (G) (H) (J)

27 (A) (B) (C) (D)

28 (F) (G) (H) (J)

29 (A) (B) (C) (D)

30 (F) (G) (H) (J)

Section 2: Reading Comprehension

50 Minutes

54 Questions

Directions: *Make sure you have a watch to time yourself and a No. 2 pencil. When you are ready, start timing yourself, and spend 50 minutes answering the questions in this section. Mark your answers on the answer sheet provided. If you are finished before the time is up, check over your work.*

Reading Comprehension

Directions

Read the passage. Then answer each question that follows.

Sample

> When Margarita heard the weather report predict a severe thunderstorm within the half hour, she began to worry how her younger brother would get home from his friend's house. Certainly he couldn't walk all those blocks in the rain.

Margarita's brother was —

- Ⓐ doing his homework in his room
- ⬤ at a friend's house
- Ⓒ playing in the backyard
- Ⓓ still at school

Annual Fall Harvest Festival

The annual Plymouth Harvest Festival will take place from October 7 to October 12. This year's festival will feature local artists, musicians, and crafters who will present their talents to the entire community. Bring your family, friends, and neighbors!

Ticket Prices

	One Day	Two Days	Three or More Days
Individual:	$5	$10	$14
Family:	$18	$20	$22

October 7–11

Main Lawn:	Hay rides, pumpkin picking, craft sale, bake sale
Sports Field:	Sack races, tag football game, art exhibition
Library:	Book reading, round table discussion, town meeting

October 12

The grand finale festival concert featuring the Plymouth Community Orchestra. This year's performance will be conducted by Roger Hamm, a graduate of the Royal Conservatory of Music.

Bring your ticket stub from any of the town summer activities and receive 10 percent off your admission to the Fall Festival.

GO ON

1 How much will you pay if you bring your family for four days?

- (A) $10
- (B) $18
- (C) $20
- (D) $22

2 Where would you *most* likely find this flyer?

- (F) a national magazine
- (G) a local store window
- (H) an encyclopedia
- (J) an almanac

3 All of the following will appear at the festival *except*—

- (A) professional athletes
- (B) orchestra musicians
- (C) talented crafters
- (D) local artists

4 On what date would you attend the festival if you wanted to see the community orchestra?

- (F) October 8
- (G) October 9
- (H) October 11
- (J) October 12

5 There is enough information on this flyer to show that—

- (A) there will be prizes awarded
- (B) the conductor is a local musician
- (C) the festival occurs every year
- (D) the library will be closed during the festival

6 All of the following will occur on the Main Lawn *except* —

- (F) art exhibition
- (G) pumpkin picking
- (H) bake sale
- (J) hay rides

7 This flyer was written to appeal to —

- (A) the library members
- (B) the entire country
- (C) the town residents
- (D) the craft society

8 What is the incentive for a person to come with the whole family?

- (F) Families get free admission to the finale concert.
- (G) The festival offers a good price package for families.
- (H) Families can join the sack race together.
- (J) The library will offer family oriented discussions.

GO ON

His Brother's Keeper

My big brother Ben was late coming home from school today. I had rushed home right after my last class. Now I sat in the kitchen, waiting for him. The grandfather clock in the living room chimed five times. Five o'clock. I shifted nervously in my chair. What was keeping him?

I admire Ben more than anyone. He swims on the school swim team in the winter, and he runs track in the spring. But the fact is that Ben is even better at school than he is at sports. I wish I were as smart as he is. He often coaches me with my math homework. One time I asked him if he ever got tired of helping me.

"Not at all, Jeremy," he said. "If the shoe were on the other foot, I know you would do the same for me." That made me feel better. Still, I never thought I would get the chance to return the favor.

But last semester, Ben had to miss an entire month of school because he was sick. When he went back to school, he had trouble concentrating on his work and catching up on everything he had missed. Even though he was not on the track team that season, he was still behind in his schoolwork.

One night he came into my room and said, "Well, Jeremy, the shoe is on the other foot." I knew exactly what he meant. "How can I help?" I asked. He asked me to coach him for his U.S. History final. It was important that he do well so he could take the advanced course next year.

Of course, I agreed. We worked every night for a week. I asked him about the dates, places, and people in his textbook. I drilled the information into his memory.

Yesterday, Ben took the test. Today, I knew he would get his grade. But where was he? Just when I thought I could not bear the suspense any longer, I heard him come in the front door. I sprang out of my chair to greet him.

He looked serious—a bad sign. "So how did you do?" I asked, trying to sound casual. "As well as I could expect," Ben said, "after being coached by the likes of you." My heart sank. But then he suddenly smiled. "I scored 94 out 100," he said. "A big fat 'A'!" He shook my hand and thanked me. But the truth is, his smile had been all the thanks I needed.

GO ON

9 When is Jeremy sitting in the kitchen?

   Ⓐ in the morning
   Ⓑ at noon
   Ⓒ at 5 in the afternoon
   Ⓓ just before dinner

10 What did Ben mean when he said, "The shoe is on the other foot"?

   Ⓕ Now he needed Jeremy's help
   Ⓖ He was too weak after being sick to put on his shoes
   Ⓗ Ben was on the track team
   Ⓙ Ben wouldn't be able to help Jeremy for a while

11 At the end of the story, Jeremy probably feels —

   Ⓐ disappointed
   Ⓑ humbled
   Ⓒ glad
   Ⓓ amused

12 Why did Jeremy need Ben's help?

   Ⓕ His worst subject was history
   Ⓖ He wanted to skip a level in history
   Ⓗ He wanted to make his younger brother feel good
   Ⓙ He was having trouble catching up on the work he missed

13 This passage is most like a —

   Ⓐ fable
   Ⓑ newspaper article
   Ⓒ mystery novel
   Ⓓ personal essay

14 When did Ben take the test?

   Ⓕ yesterday
   Ⓖ a week ago
   Ⓗ that day
   Ⓙ two weeks ago

15 When Ben finally comes home after learning his test score, he tries to —

   Ⓐ fool Jeremy
   Ⓑ avoid Jeremy
   Ⓒ act casual
   Ⓓ hide his disappointment

16 How did Jeremy feel about helping Ben?

   Ⓕ honored
   Ⓖ bored
   Ⓗ resentful
   Ⓙ stressed

GO ON

Works Cited

Bando, Celia. *Art from Everyday Objects*. Brooklyn: Creative Link Books, 1996.

Lamdon, Mark. *Art for the Teenage Artist*. Oakland: Arts Press, 1994.

Parker, Paula. "Stencils You Already Own" *Creative House Play* 15 December 1998: 17–20.

Roas, Carla. "Reuse! Recycle! Recreate!" *Journal of Environmental Art* 6 April 1997. Online. Creative WebServer. 10 April 1997: 14–19.

Louiz, Paul. "Make Your Own Paper" *Boston Sunday Globe* 12 May 1998, sec B12.

United States Department of Artistic Education. *Prerequisites for Entry into Art Colleges*. Washington: University Standard Press, 1997.

GO ON

17 What source would you use if you were interested in applying to California Art Institute?

- (A) *Art for the Teenage Artist*
- (B) *Prerequisites for Entry into Art Colleges*
- (C) *Journal of Environmental Art*
- (D) *Creative House Play*

18 Which of these entries was a result of Internet research?

- (F) "Stencils You Already Own"
- (G) "Make Your Own Paper"
- (H) *Art for the Teenage Artist*
- (J) "Reuse! Recycle! Recreate!"

19 Which of these sources would *not* be good to use if you were looking for information on art for which you didn't need to buy a lot of supplies?

- (A) "Reuse! Recycle! Recreate!"
- (B) *Art for the Teenage Artist*
- (C) "Stencils You Already Own"
- (D) *Art From Everyday Objects*

20 Who probably knows the most about where to buy the metal screens you need to make paper?

- (F) Paul Louiz
- (G) Mark Lamdon
- (H) Paula Parker
- (J) Carla Roas

21 Which text does *not* list an author?

- (A) "Stencils You Already Own"
- (B) *Art from Everyday Objects*
- (C) *Prerequisites for Entry into Art Colleges*
- (D) "Reuse! Recycle! Recreate!"

GO ON

A Bright Idea

Thomas Edison was born in Milan, Ohio in 1847. As a boy he was very curious and showed a fierce interest in science. He grew up to become a world-famous inventor. In fact, modern life would not be possible without the inventions of Thomas Edison.

On September 4, 1882, a crowd of people gathered at Edison's new Pearl Street power station in New York City. Edison, the "Wizard of Menlo Park," stood ready to flip the main switch that would start up the power station. When the station started working, some 800 electric lamps in 25 nearby office buildings would suddenly light up for the first time.

Edison had long dreamed of this moment. He was sure that people needed the electric light bulb. He would give it to them safely, cheaply. It would make their lives better and make him a rich man. He was confident of that.

But many in the crowd were not so sure. Nothing like this had ever been done before. Edison had struggled for years just to invent the light bulb itself. So had some of the greatest scientists in the world. They all had failed.

By the late 1870's, Edison had fit together some important pieces of the puzzle. He knew that a successful electric lamp should be a closed glass tube, or bulb. All the air should be pumped out of the bulb, creating a vacuum inside it. Also inside would be a thin wire or filament. When electric current passed through the filament, it would become glowing hot and give off light.

The problem was, the current created too much heat. The thin filament wire always melted. Edison tried making filaments out of a thousand different materials, from fine gold thread to human hair. Most of them burned up within a few seconds. A few lasted several minutes, none more than a few hours. A filament made of platinum lasted the longest. But platinum is a rare metal and very expensive. One of Edison's men calculated that each light bulb made of platinum would cost nearly one hundred dollars!

Finally, in October, 1879, Edison had an inspiration. He took a simple piece of cotton thread and burned it. The burning covered the thread with a layer of charred carbon. The first bulb with this filament inside it glowed steadily for fifteen hours!

It was one thing to develop a practical light bulb. Now Edison needed to make thousands of such bulbs. He built a factory to do just that. He needed a power station, too, and miles of electrical cable to run current from the power station into those office buildings. Edison worked day and night for almost three years on the project, and so did the hundreds of men he employed.

And now, at last, the moment was at hand. The crowd held its breath. Edison threw the switch. The power plant hummed into action. Then, a louder sound came from out in the streets. It was the sound of people shouting. They stared in amazement at the electric lamps glowing in the windows of those lucky office buildings, and they shouted Thomas Edison's name.

GO ON

22 Edison built the Pearl Street power station to—

F manufacture light bulbs
G generate electrical current
H manufacture electrical cable
J design vacuum pumps

23 Why were people shouting in the streets?

A Edison had designed a successful filament.
B Edison had made New York famous.
C The power station made too much noise.
D The office buildings had just lit up.

24 This essay was written mainly in order to—

F explain why electricity is important
G show how a mystery was solved
H describe one man's great achievement
J celebrate scientific progress

25 There is enough information in Paragraph 3 to show that—

A Edison wanted to make money from electricity
B the public believed that Edison would succeed
C no one wanted Edison's invention
D Edison doubted his own abilities

26 This essay would most likely be found in a book titled—

F *Famous Scientific Hoaxes*
G *The Great Inventor*
H *A History of New York City*
J *The Uses of Carbon*

27 The filament that was most successful was made out of—

A gold
B hair
C platinum
D thread

28 There is enough information in Paragraph 4 to suggest that Edison—

F worked with famous scientists
G was unpopular
H competed against other inventors
J succeeded quickly where others failed

29 If the author added another paragraph after Paragraph 9, it would probably tell—

A what happened to the Pearl Street power station
B what Edison's family life was like
C how Edison followed up his Pearl Street success
D why electricity can be dangerous

GO ON

Rabbit and the River

Rabbit needed to cross the river, but the rush of water was too fast. The cold water looked very menacing to Rabbit, and he shivered at the thought of trying to swim across it. But Mongoose, who was nervous to begin with, would worry if Rabbit did not get back to the meadow on time. Several meadow animals had disappeared over the last two moons. They were beginning to think that a predator—perhaps Bear?—had decided to start eating them. Bear lived by himself up in the mountains. He wasn't a meadow creature like Mongoose or Rabbit.

Suddenly, Bear crashed out of the forest, right behind Rabbit. Rabbit made an instant decision: He dove head first into the river. The rough water immediately swept Rabbit down the river. He tried to swim, but the current was too strong. Bear bounded into the river, caught up to Rabbit, and grabbed him with his big paw. Rabbit was confused and terrified. "Don't worry," Bear told him, "I only like fish." Bear winked at Rabbit and gently carried him to the other side of the river. Rabbit felt ashamed that he had suspected Bear of eating his fellow animals.

Bear carried Rabbit all the way back to the meadow. When Mongoose saw Rabbit cradled in Bear's arms, she was stunned. She had never seen anything like it in all her moons. It occurred to her that Bear had never been anything but nice to all of the animals she knew (except the fish). Mongoose felt ashamed that she had suspected Bear. Like Rabbit, she had learned to avoid rushing to judgment.

GO ON

30 According to the first paragraph, what has happened "over the last two moons"?

 (F) food supply has dwindled
 (G) the water has become colder
 (H) several animals have disappeared
 (J) Mongoose has become nervous

31 Why was Rabbit confused and terrified?

 (A) because the water was too cold
 (B) because Bear only liked fish
 (C) because Bear jumped in the river and grabbed Rabbit
 (D) because the food supply had dwindled

32 There is enough information in the passage to show that—

 (F) Mongoose will be very nice to Bear next time they meet
 (G) food supply will come back before the next moon
 (H) Rabbit should have waited to cross the river
 (J) this story takes place in September

GO ON

FALL FESTIVAL

Where: The Public Center Park
(excluding Farm Pasture and Pointe Green)

When: Sunday October 3rd—One Day Only!

Cost: A can of food for our Fall Food Drive

Note: The park will also be available for normal weekend use in areas not assigned to the Fall Festival.

Schedule of Events:

ADULTS	11 AM	1 PM	2:30 PM
what	Brunch	Jazz	Rollerblade demonstration
where	Picnic Area	underneath the Willow Tree	Esplanade

TEENS	11 AM	1 PM	2:30 PM
what	Rollerblade demonstration	Lunch	HS Rock Group *Mr. Cool*
where	Picnic Area	Main Lawn	Baseball Field

KIDS	11 AM	1 PM	2:30 PM
what	Children's Theater	Lunch	Face painting
where	underneath the Willow Tree	Gazebo	underneath the Willow Tree

GO ON

33 Which activity location is used twice for the same group of people?

    (A)   the Esplanade
    (B)   underneath the Willow Tree
    (C)   the Gazebo
    (D)   the Picnic Area

34 What will the teens be doing at 1 P.M.?

    (F)   having lunch
    (G)   watching a roller blading demonstration
    (H)   listening to a Rock Band
    (J)   listening to a Jazz Band

35 What section of the park will *not* be used on Sunday, October 3?

    (A)   the Baseball Field
    (B)   the Picnic Area
    (C)   Pointe Green
    (D)   the Esplanade

36 If you go to the Gazebo at 1 P.M., what will you be doing?

    (F)   having lunch with the kids
    (G)   listening to jazz with the adults
    (H)   watching rollerblading with the teens
    (J)   listening to music with the teens

37 What will the adults be doing at 2:30?

    (A)   seeing a play
    (B)   listening to Jazz
    (C)   eating lunch
    (D)   watching a rollerblading demonstration

38 How can you get into the Festival?

    (F)   just walk in
    (G)   pay $5.00
    (H)   bring a can of food
    (J)   with a parent

39 What will the teens probably be sitting on when they watch *Mr. Cool* play?

    (A)   picnic benches
    (B)   pavement
    (C)   pool chairs
    (D)   bleachers

40 What will probably happen if you come to the Fall Festival on Saturday, October 2?

    (F)   you'll need 2 cans to get in
    (G)   the Fall Festival won't be there
    (H)   the park will be closed
    (J)   the pool will be open

GO ON

The Basics of Fishing

Materials You Will Need:

a fishing rod	cooler for the fish
fishing wire	sunscreen
live bait (preferably worms)	hat
hooks	patience
tackle box	

Procedures:

Note: You may want to consult an experienced fisherman before your first outing.

First, thread the fishing wire through your rod so that the wire is tightly wound.
Second, attach the live bait to the hook.
Third, cast your line and slowly reel the wire in.
Finally, sit back, relax, and wait for the fish to bite.

Tips:

When a fish bites, do not jerk the line.
Do not get frustrated. It takes years to become a good fisherman.
Make sure you wear your hat and sunscreen.

Kay's Fish Market

Best Fish Restaurant in Town

Filet of Flounder
This delicious fish features Kay's best catch of flounder. Served over rice and vegetables. A house favorite.

Lobster Bisque
Winner of the East Coast Fish Mongers Award in 1994. This tasty soup will entice your taste buds with giant pieces of lobster.

Rachel's Seafood Stew
A superb mixture of shrimp, scallops, and lobster served with fresh herbs and spices. Served over fresh pasta.

Lobster Dinner for Two
More lobster than you can handle! Fresh from the coast, these lobsters are the meatiest anywhere in town.

Blackened Catfish Sandwich
This dish features New Orleans spices on a fresh piece of catfish. Grilled, fried, or baked. Served on fresh bread.

Have **Kay's Fish Market** cater your next party. Speak to Fred, the manager, for more details. Cash only. No credit cards or personal checks.

GO ON

41 According to *The Basics of Fishing,* what should you do after you attach the live bait to the hook?

- Ⓐ wait for the fish to bite
- Ⓑ cast your line
- Ⓒ thread the fishing wire
- Ⓓ put on sunscreen

42 Which of these dishes at *Kay's Fish Market* is a soup?

- Ⓕ Rachel's Seafood Stew
- Ⓖ Filet of Flounder
- Ⓗ Lobster Bisque
- Ⓙ Blackened Catfish Sandwich

43 How could you pay for your meal at *Kay's Fish Market*?

- Ⓐ cash, credit card, or personal check
- Ⓑ cash only
- Ⓒ credit card only
- Ⓓ the passage does not say

44 Which of these does *The Basics of Fishing* not say you need to go fishing?

- Ⓕ some hooks
- Ⓖ live bait
- Ⓗ a rod
- Ⓙ a boat

45 Where might you find *The Basics of Fishing*?

- Ⓐ an encyclopedia
- Ⓑ a sports history book
- Ⓒ a sports magazine
- Ⓓ a catalogue of supplies

GO ON

Tumbleweed

I found Tumbleweed in a haystack in the barn. He was a very small baby mouse—so young that his eyes were still closed. I don't know how he had been separated from his mother, but he was all alone when I found him. Since he didn't have his mother, we were not able to give him the kind of milk that he was used to. My Mom and I heated up some milk and fed it to Tumbleweed with an eyedropper. At night, Tumbleweed would make small noises while he slept. I could tell that Tumbleweed was trying hard to stay alive and that he was very dependent on me.

At first, Tumbleweed seemed to be getting weaker and weaker. His eyes did not open for a long time and he was not eating very much. My mother tried to warn me that he may not survive without his mother, but I kept feeding him and caring for him.

I woke up one morning about a week later to a very heartening sight. There was Tumbleweed, staring up at me. He seemed to be much stronger; he even ate some small bits of lettuce from my hand.

When Tumbleweed was strong enough, I brought him back to the barn where I had found him. I knew that I couldn't keep him in the house and that he would be happier if living with the other mice on the farm. I said good-bye to him and put him back on the haystack. I was sad, but I knew I was doing the right thing by letting him go free.

GO ON

KAPLAN

46 There is enough information to show that this story takes place—

- Ⓕ in the very distant past
- Ⓖ on a farm
- Ⓗ a city
- Ⓙ in the future

47 Why were Tumbleweed's eyes closed when the narrator found him?

- Ⓐ It was too light in the barn for his eyes to stay open
- Ⓑ He was dreaming
- Ⓒ He was too young for them to have opened yet
- Ⓓ He was very sick

48 According to the story, what would have been the most likely explanation if Tumbleweed had not survived?

- Ⓕ The narrator didn't take good care of him
- Ⓖ He didn't like being kept in a house
- Ⓗ He needed to be around other mice to get healthy
- Ⓙ He couldn't survive without his mother

49 The best way to learn more about raising animals who have lost their mothers would be to—

- Ⓐ ask a friend
- Ⓑ look in the encyclopedia under "Animals"
- Ⓒ read a book about animal development
- Ⓓ visit a farm

50 What was the *first* sign that Tumblweed was feeling better?

- Ⓕ he was staring at the narrator
- Ⓖ he made noises while he slept
- Ⓗ he kept running towards the barn
- Ⓙ he was able to find food on his own

GO ON

Music Bibliography

Edenburg, Leslie. "The Five Greatest Composers of All Time." *Music Digest* 8 April 1994: 12–18.

Greene, Maxine. *Music and Life: How Music Helps Us Live*. New York: Arco, 1998.

Harley, David, ed. *Music Dictionary for Students*. Chicago: River, 1982.

Killburn, Kathy. "Why Children Like Music." *Journal of Childhood Music* 9 June 1990: 16–19.

"Music" *The Arts Encyclopedia Online*. Online [www.artscyc.com]. 15 June 1996.

"Music: Does It Make Children Smarter?" *Los Angeles Review* 1 November 1992: A14.

Nevada State Report on Music Learning. *Music in the Schools*. Preston, Nevada: School Press, 1996.

GO ON

51 In the bibliography, titles of books are —

- (A) underlined
- (B) in bold
- (C) in italics
- (D) in quotation marks

52 Which author would you interview if you wanted to know more about the relationship between children and music?

- (F) Leslie Edenburg
- (G) Maxine Greene
- (H) David Harley, ed.
- (J) Kathy Killburn

53 Where would you go if you wanted to learn more about musical terminology?

- (A) *Music Dictionary for Students*
- (B) *Music in the Schools*
- (C) *The Arts Encyclopedia Online*
- (D) "The Five Greatest Composers of All Time"

54 Which of the bibliography entries was published in Chicago?

- (F) *Music Digest 8*
- (G) *Music Dictionary for Students*
- (H) *Music in the Schools*
- (J) *Music and Life: How Music Helps Us Live*

STOP

Answer Sheet

1	Ⓐ	Ⓑ	Ⓒ	Ⓓ
2	Ⓕ	Ⓖ	Ⓗ	Ⓙ
3	Ⓐ	Ⓑ	Ⓒ	Ⓓ
4	Ⓕ	Ⓖ	Ⓗ	Ⓙ
5	Ⓐ	Ⓑ	Ⓒ	Ⓓ
6	Ⓕ	Ⓖ	Ⓗ	Ⓙ
7	Ⓐ	Ⓑ	Ⓒ	Ⓓ
8	Ⓕ	Ⓖ	Ⓗ	Ⓙ
9	Ⓐ	Ⓑ	Ⓒ	Ⓓ
10	Ⓕ	Ⓖ	Ⓗ	Ⓙ
11	Ⓐ	Ⓑ	Ⓒ	Ⓓ
12	Ⓕ	Ⓖ	Ⓗ	Ⓙ
13	Ⓐ	Ⓑ	Ⓒ	Ⓓ
14	Ⓕ	Ⓖ	Ⓗ	Ⓙ
15	Ⓐ	Ⓑ	Ⓒ	Ⓓ
16	Ⓕ	Ⓖ	Ⓗ	Ⓙ
17	Ⓐ	Ⓑ	Ⓒ	Ⓓ
18	Ⓕ	Ⓖ	Ⓗ	Ⓙ
19	Ⓐ	Ⓑ	Ⓒ	Ⓓ
20	Ⓕ	Ⓖ	Ⓗ	Ⓙ
21	Ⓐ	Ⓑ	Ⓒ	Ⓓ
22	Ⓕ	Ⓖ	Ⓗ	Ⓙ
23	Ⓐ	Ⓑ	Ⓒ	Ⓓ
24	Ⓕ	Ⓖ	Ⓗ	Ⓙ
25	Ⓐ	Ⓑ	Ⓒ	Ⓓ
26	Ⓕ	Ⓖ	Ⓗ	Ⓙ
27	Ⓐ	Ⓑ	Ⓒ	Ⓓ
28	Ⓕ	Ⓖ	Ⓗ	Ⓙ
29	Ⓐ	Ⓑ	Ⓒ	Ⓓ
30	Ⓕ	Ⓖ	Ⓗ	Ⓙ
31	Ⓐ	Ⓑ	Ⓒ	Ⓓ
32	Ⓕ	Ⓖ	Ⓗ	Ⓙ
33	Ⓐ	Ⓑ	Ⓒ	Ⓓ
34	Ⓕ	Ⓖ	Ⓗ	Ⓙ
35	Ⓐ	Ⓑ	Ⓒ	Ⓓ
36	Ⓕ	Ⓖ	Ⓗ	Ⓙ
37	Ⓐ	Ⓑ	Ⓒ	Ⓓ
38	Ⓕ	Ⓖ	Ⓗ	Ⓙ
39	Ⓐ	Ⓑ	Ⓒ	Ⓓ
40	Ⓕ	Ⓖ	Ⓗ	Ⓙ
41	Ⓐ	Ⓑ	Ⓒ	Ⓓ
42	Ⓕ	Ⓖ	Ⓗ	Ⓙ
43	Ⓐ	Ⓑ	Ⓒ	Ⓓ
44	Ⓕ	Ⓖ	Ⓗ	Ⓙ
45	Ⓐ	Ⓑ	Ⓒ	Ⓓ
46	Ⓕ	Ⓖ	Ⓗ	Ⓙ
47	Ⓐ	Ⓑ	Ⓒ	Ⓓ
48	Ⓕ	Ⓖ	Ⓗ	Ⓙ
49	Ⓐ	Ⓑ	Ⓒ	Ⓓ
50	Ⓕ	Ⓖ	Ⓗ	Ⓙ
51	Ⓐ	Ⓑ	Ⓒ	Ⓓ
52	Ⓕ	Ⓖ	Ⓗ	Ⓙ
53	Ⓐ	Ⓑ	Ⓒ	Ⓓ
54	Ⓕ	Ⓖ	Ⓗ	Ⓙ

Section 3: Math— Problem Solving

50 Minutes

52 Questions

Directions: *Make sure you have a watch to time yourself, a No. 2 pencil, and a ruler that has both metric and standard units. Use of a standard calculator is also permitted. When you are ready, start timing yourself, and spend 50 minutes answering the questions in this section. Mark your answers on the answer sheet provided. If you are finished before the time is up, check over your work.*

Mathematics— Problem Solving

Directions

Read each question and select the best answer. Then mark the space for the answer you selected.

Sample

The planet Mercury is about 5.8×10^7 km from the sun. What number is represented by 5.8×10^7?

Ⓐ 5,800
Ⓑ 580,000
Ⓒ 5,800,000
⬤ 58,000,000

1 Margaret went to the grocery store and bought $45.91 worth of groceries. Then she went to the pharmacy and spent $6.00 to have a prescription filled. Finally, she went to the pizza parlor and bought a large pizza pie for $12.35. How much money did she spend all together?

Ⓐ $64.26
Ⓑ $64.46
Ⓒ $78.36
Ⓓ $150.06

2 Javier is taking a trip to the beach. He is taking $900 with him. The hotel he is staying at costs $78 a night. If he is staying at the hotel for 4 nights, how much will it cost him?

Ⓕ $78
Ⓖ $312
Ⓗ $322
Ⓙ $900

3 The highest score Maureen could have gotten on her math test was 100. If 19 points were subtracted from her test score for questions she answered incorrectly, what score did Maureen receive on her test?

Ⓐ 119
Ⓑ 91
Ⓒ 86
Ⓓ 81

4 A movie started at 7:55 P.M. If it lasted for $2\frac{1}{2}$ hours, what time did the movie end?

Ⓕ 9:25 P.M.
Ⓖ 10:15 P.M.
Ⓗ 10:25 P.M.
Ⓙ 10:55 P.M.

GO ON

KAPLAN

5 Jennifer bought a box in which to store her family photos.

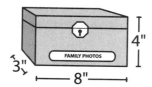

FAMILY PHOTOS

4"

3"

8"

Use $V = l \times w \times h$ to determine the volume of the box. What is the volume?

- Ⓐ 16 cu. inches
- Ⓑ 24 cu. inches
- Ⓒ 32 cu. inches
- Ⓓ 96 cu. inches

6 Joey, Shelley, and Derek each ate 1 hamburger and 1 order of french fries. How much money did they spend on food all together?

Food	Cost
Hamburger	$1.75
French Fries	$0.85

- Ⓕ $7.75
- Ⓖ $7.80
- Ⓗ $10.00
- Ⓙ $17.75

7 The table below shows how much money Andre earned mowing lawns for three summers.

Summer, 1997	$100.50
Summer, 1998	$160.25
Summer, 1999	$205.75

How much more money did Andre earn mowing lawns in the summer of 1999 than he earned in the summer of 1997?

- Ⓐ $45.50
- Ⓑ $105.25
- Ⓒ $115.75
- Ⓓ $205.75

8 This card is taken from a card catalog. The reference number for this book is in the upper right corner.

```
                                    513.642

Stewart, Mark. Math for Smart Test-Takers.
New York, NY: Macmillan, USA
c. 1998
```

What is the value corresponding to the 4 in this number?

- Ⓕ 4 thousandths
- Ⓖ 4 hundredths
- Ⓗ 4 tenths
- Ⓙ 4

GO ON

9 Each ⬜ represents 0.1.

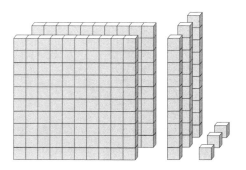

What number is pictured above?

(A) 2,330

(B) 233

(C) 23.3

(D) 2.33

10 An astronomical unit, the distance between the earth and the sun, is 9.30×10^7 miles. What number is represented by 9.30×10^7?

(F) 93,000

(G) 930,000

(H) 9,300,000

(J) 93,000,000

11 In the equation $y = x^2$, what is the value of y when $x = 3$?

(A) 6

(B) 9

(C) 12

(D) 27

12 The perimeter of a table is found by $P = 2l + 2w$, where l is the length of the table and w is the width. If $l = 3$ and $w = 1$, what is the perimeter of the table?

(F) 6

(G) 7

(H) 8

(J) 10

13 The cost of tolls on the state highway is \$0.25 per mile, plus \$5 for the bridge. The total cost (T) of a trip is found by the equation $T = 0.25m + 5$, where m is the number of miles traveled. If the Green family travels 40 miles, what is the total cost of their toll charges?

(A) \$6

(B) \$15

(C) \$45.25

(D) \$1005

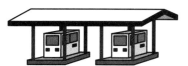

14 The rate, r, in kilometers per hour, is the distance, d, divided by the time, t. ($r = \frac{d}{t}$). If Halle walks 12 kilometers in 2 hours, what is her rate?

(F) 3 km/hr

(G) 6 km/hr

(H) 10 km/hr

(J) 14 km/hr

GO ON

15 In the equation $v = 3g + 2$, what is the value of v when g is 4?

(A) 9
(B) 12
(C) 14
(D) 18

16 The number machine below follows a rule that changes numbers into other numbers in the same way each time.

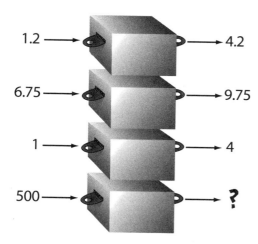

What number will 500 be changed into?

(F) 500.2
(G) 502.75
(H) 503
(J) 506

17 If a typist can type 2 pages of text every 5 minutes, then at this rate, how many hours will it take to type 100 pages of text?

(A) $3\frac{3}{4}$ hours
(B) $4\frac{1}{10}$ hours
(C) $4\frac{1}{6}$ hours
(D) $4\frac{3}{4}$ hours

18 How many cans are in this stack?

(F) 140
(G) 135
(H) 49
(J) 2,520

GO ON

19 Kathy commutes from Santa Monica to downtown L.A. She recorded the following travel times last week.

Day	Minutes
Monday	22.3
Tuesday	19.6
Wednesday	25.7
Thursday	28.2
Friday	23.9

What was Kathy's mean travel time last week?

- (A) 17.13
- (B) 23.9
- (C) 23.94
- (D) 29.32

20 What is the mode of the long jump results listed below?

Student	Long Jump Results
John	12 feet 5 inches
Mark	9 feet 7 inches
Chris	10 feet 4 inches
Bob	12 feet 5 inches
Mike	9 feet 2 inches
Jahan	10 feet 5 inches

- (F) 10 feet 4 inches
- (G) 10 feet 5 inches
- (H) 11 feet 1 inch
- (J) 12 feet 5 inches

GO ON

21 100 people were asked to name a favorite juice. Based on the pie chart below, which juice do you think only 5 people named as a favorite?

Distribution of Favorite Juice Flavors of 100 People

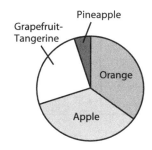

Ⓐ Apple
Ⓑ Grapefruit tangerine
Ⓒ Pineapple
Ⓓ Orange

22 Which represents the coordinates of the upper right hand corner of the square?

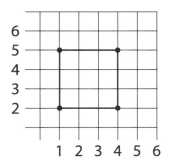

Ⓕ (5, 1)
Ⓖ (2, 1)
Ⓗ (4, 2)
Ⓙ (4, 5)

23 Which represents the coordinates of Point A?

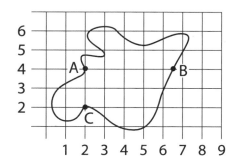

Ⓐ (2, 2)
Ⓑ (4, 2)
Ⓒ (2, 4)
Ⓓ (5, 3)

24 The price of Baymore stock was how much higher than Amcor stock during the month of April?

STOCK PRICES IN DOLLARS

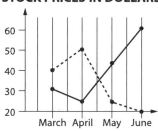

——— Amcor Stock
------- Baymore Stock

Ⓕ $20
Ⓖ $25
Ⓗ $30
Ⓙ $35

GO ON

25 About how much earlier than Danton did the population of Argville reach 12,000?

CITY POPULATIONS 1950–1990

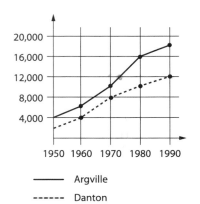

- —— Argville
- ------ Danton

- (A) 5 years
- (B) 10 years
- (C) 15 years
- (D) 25 years

26 If the amount of a discount between peak and offpeak ticket prices is always in the same range, what price would you expect to pay for an offpeak ticket from Seattle to Portland?

	WEEKDAY		WEEKEND	
	Peak	Offpeak	Peak	Offpeak
New York–Boston	92	78	98	82
L. A.–San Francisco	124	110	135	120
Orlando–Miami	65	49	68	54
Washington, D.C.–Durham	137	123	145	131
Seattle–Portland	81	67	87	

- (F) $45
- (G) $60
- (H) $72
- (J) $87

27 If the cost of a three-day rental divided by the cost of a one-day rental is the same in all cities, how much would you expect to pay to rent a car for three days in Aspen?

Length of Rental	L. A.	Oakland	Aspen
1 day	54	32	78
3 days	108	64	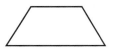
5 days	215	135	310
10 days	425	265	600

- (A) $40
- (B) $78
- (C) $100
- (D) $156

28 Which statement about the angles of this trapezoid is true?

- (F) All four angles seem to be right angles.
- (G) Two angles appear to be acute and two angles appear to be obtuse.
- (H) Two angles seem to be right angles and two angles seem to be acute.
- (J) Two angles seem to be right angles, one angle appears to be acute, and one angle appears to be obtuse.

GO ON

29 Susanna bought a tool box in which to store her tools.

1 ft
2 ft
3 ft

What is the volume of the tool box? (Use $V = l\,w\,h$.)

- Ⓐ 4 cu ft
- Ⓑ 6 cu ft
- Ⓒ 7 cu ft
- Ⓓ 8 cu ft

30

The straight edges where both cuts were made in the pizza pie pictured above are both good models of

- Ⓕ a radius
- Ⓖ an arc
- Ⓗ a sector
- Ⓙ a diameter

31 Approximately how many inches will this unicycle travel if the diameter of the wheel is 20 inches and the wheel completes one revolution?

- Ⓐ 3.14
- Ⓑ 31.4
- Ⓒ 62.8
- Ⓓ 628

32 The lane dividers in the Creek Valley School pool are a good example of —

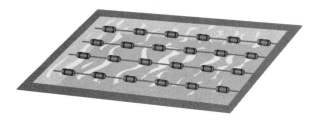

- Ⓕ intersecting lines
- Ⓖ a diameter
- Ⓗ a perimeter
- Ⓙ parallel lines

33 What kind of polygon has eight sides?

- Ⓐ pentagon
- Ⓑ hexagon
- Ⓒ octagon
- Ⓓ septagon

GO ON

34 Sammy's grandparents store their record albums in this box.

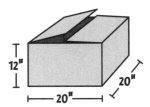

What is the volume of the box?
(Use *V = l w h*.)

- Ⓕ 3600 cu in
- Ⓖ 4000 cu in
- Ⓗ 4800 cu in
- Ⓙ 5200 cu in

35 Which figure has the least area?

Ⓐ

Ⓑ

Ⓒ

Ⓓ

36 How much fabric is needed to make this flag to be flown on the mast of a ship?

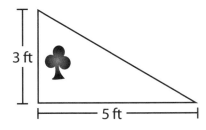

(Use *A = ½ bh*.)

- Ⓕ 5 sq ft
- Ⓖ 6.5 sq ft
- Ⓗ 7.5 sq ft
- Ⓙ 8.75 sq ft

37 The temperature in the mountains was –10° Celsius last week. If the temperature rises by 10° this week, what will the temperature be?

- Ⓐ –20° Celsius
- Ⓑ 0° Celsius
- Ⓒ 10° Celsius
- Ⓓ 20° Celsius

GO ON

38 The swimming pool is marked at the edge so that you know how deep the water is in that section of the pool. The pool deepens gradually and there is a person swimming in the section of the pool where the arrow is pointing.

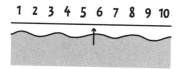

Which is closest to the depth of the water where the person is swimming?

F $5\frac{1}{8}$

G $5\frac{2}{3}$

H $6\frac{1}{8}$

J $6\frac{2}{3}$

39 The highest score that Lian could get on her test was 100. Her teacher took 14 points off of her test for the questions Lian answered incorrectly. What score did Lian get on her test?

A 114

B 100

C 86

D 84

40 Sammy decided to measure the tides. 0 marks the level where the water is between tides. The area above the 0 measures the level of the water at high tide and the area below the 0 measures the level of the water at low tide.

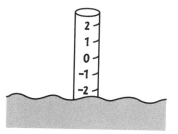

Which is closest to the current level of the water?

F $-3\frac{1}{4}$

G $-2\frac{1}{2}$

H $-2\frac{7}{8}$

J $2\frac{3}{4}$

41 The average temperature for the month of January in Fairbanks, Alaska is –13° Fahrenheit. In April, the average temperature in Fairbanks is 43°F warmer than that. What is the average temperature in April?

A 43°

B 30°

C 26°

D –56°

GO ON

42 A millipede measures 0.6763 centimeters.

0.6763 cm

What is that number rounded to the nearest thousandth?

- Ⓕ 0.700
- Ⓖ 0.670
- Ⓗ 0.676
- Ⓙ 0.600

43 Roger weighs 144 $\frac{7}{16}$ pounds

144 $\frac{7}{16}$ pounds

What is that number of pounds rounded to the nearest whole number?

- Ⓐ 144
- Ⓑ 144 $\frac{1}{2}$
- Ⓒ 145
- Ⓓ 146

44 The distance from Paul's house to Jill's house is 3 $\frac{1}{3}$ miles.

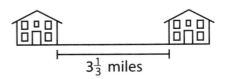

3 $\frac{1}{3}$ miles

What is that distance rounded to the nearest quarter-mile?

- Ⓕ 3 miles
- Ⓖ 3 $\frac{1}{4}$ miles
- Ⓗ 3 $\frac{1}{2}$ miles
- Ⓙ 3 $\frac{3}{4}$ miles

45 In a recent poll, 73% of the student body preferred pizza to hamburgers.

Which fraction is closest to 73%?

- Ⓐ $\frac{1}{73}$
- Ⓑ $\frac{3}{7}$
- Ⓒ $\frac{2}{3}$
- Ⓓ $\frac{3}{4}$

GO ON

KAPLAN

46 A ruler is marked off in inches to measure the length of a fish caught in the lake.

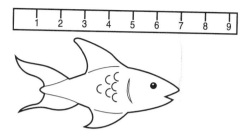

What is the closest length of that fish?

- (F) $7\frac{7}{8}$
- (G) $7\frac{3}{8}$
- (H) $8\frac{5}{8}$
- (J) $7\frac{1}{6}$

47 Randy and his friend Patrick compared their grade point average (mean) over the course of the four quarters of the school year. The graph shows their grade point averages over the course of the year.

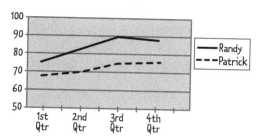

About **how many points higher is Randy's grade point average than Patrick's at the end of the 4th quarter?**

- (A) 13
- (B) 7
- (C) 10
- (D) 20

48 Alyssa is one year old. She takes a nap every afternoon. Today she woke up from her nap at 2:30 P.M. What else would you need to know to figure out how long Alyssa's nap lasted?

- (F) The name of Alyssa's mom
- (G) When Alyssa had her last bottle
- (H) What time Alyssa began to nap
- (J) What toys Alyssa has in her crib

GO ON

49 Mrs. Wu gives English, spelling, reading and writing homework every night. She always puts the homework on the board in a particular order. She never puts the writing or spelling homework first. She never puts the spelling, writing, or English homework last. She never puts the English or writing homework second. In what order does she put the homework on the board?

(A) English, spelling, reading, writing
(B) English, spelling, writing, reading
(C) Spelling, writing, English, reading
(D) Reading, English, writing, spelling

50 Diana buys a basket of peaches at the farmers' market. After she buys the basket, she has $9.00 left. What would you need to know to figure out how much she paid for the basket of peaches?

(F) How many peaches are in a basket
(G) What kind of peaches Diana bought
(H) How long it took Diana to get to the farmers' market
(J) How much money Diana had before she bought the peaches

51 Cousins Valerie, Gina, Pete, and Jimmy all take turns playing a video game. Gina and Valerie do not play first. Jimmy, Valerie, and Pete do not play second. Valerie and Jimmy do not play last. In what order do they play the video game?

(A) Valerie, Gina, Pete, Jimmy
(B) Gina, Valerie, Jimmy, Pete
(C) Jimmy, Gina, Valerie, Pete
(D) Jimmy, Gina, Pete, Valerie

52 Mrs. Hawkins is taking her class on four field trips this year: to the museum, to the theater, to the city hall, and to the planetarium. She has already decided the order in which her class will take the trips. She will not take her class to the city hall or the museum first. She will not take her class to the museum or the planetarium last. She will not take her class to the theater, the museum or the planetarium second.

(F) planetarium, city hall, museum, theater
(G) city hall, planetarium, museum, theater
(H) museum, city hall, theater, planetarium
(J) museum, city hall, planetarium, theater

STOP

Answer Sheet

1	Ⓐ	Ⓑ	Ⓒ	Ⓓ
2	Ⓕ	Ⓖ	Ⓗ	Ⓙ
3	Ⓐ	Ⓑ	Ⓒ	Ⓓ
4	Ⓕ	Ⓖ	Ⓗ	Ⓙ
5	Ⓐ	Ⓑ	Ⓒ	Ⓓ
6	Ⓕ	Ⓖ	Ⓗ	Ⓙ
7	Ⓐ	Ⓑ	Ⓒ	Ⓓ
8	Ⓕ	Ⓖ	Ⓗ	Ⓙ
9	Ⓐ	Ⓑ	Ⓒ	Ⓓ
10	Ⓕ	Ⓖ	Ⓗ	Ⓙ
11	Ⓐ	Ⓑ	Ⓒ	Ⓓ
12	Ⓕ	Ⓖ	Ⓗ	Ⓙ
13	Ⓐ	Ⓑ	Ⓒ	Ⓓ
14	Ⓕ	Ⓖ	Ⓗ	Ⓙ
15	Ⓐ	Ⓑ	Ⓒ	Ⓓ
16	Ⓕ	Ⓖ	Ⓗ	Ⓙ
17	Ⓐ	Ⓑ	Ⓒ	Ⓓ
18	Ⓕ	Ⓖ	Ⓗ	Ⓙ
19	Ⓐ	Ⓑ	Ⓒ	Ⓓ
20	Ⓕ	Ⓖ	Ⓗ	Ⓙ
21	Ⓐ	Ⓑ	Ⓒ	Ⓓ
22	Ⓕ	Ⓖ	Ⓗ	Ⓙ
23	Ⓐ	Ⓑ	Ⓒ	Ⓓ
24	Ⓕ	Ⓖ	Ⓗ	Ⓙ
25	Ⓐ	Ⓑ	Ⓒ	Ⓓ
26	Ⓕ	Ⓖ	Ⓗ	Ⓙ
27	Ⓐ	Ⓑ	Ⓒ	Ⓓ
28	Ⓕ	Ⓖ	Ⓗ	Ⓙ
29	Ⓐ	Ⓑ	Ⓒ	Ⓓ
30	Ⓕ	Ⓖ	Ⓗ	Ⓙ
31	Ⓐ	Ⓑ	Ⓒ	Ⓓ
32	Ⓕ	Ⓖ	Ⓗ	Ⓙ
33	Ⓐ	Ⓑ	Ⓒ	Ⓓ
34	Ⓕ	Ⓖ	Ⓗ	Ⓙ
35	Ⓐ	Ⓑ	Ⓒ	Ⓓ
36	Ⓕ	Ⓖ	Ⓗ	Ⓙ
37	Ⓐ	Ⓑ	Ⓒ	Ⓓ
38	Ⓕ	Ⓖ	Ⓗ	Ⓙ
39	Ⓐ	Ⓑ	Ⓒ	Ⓓ
40	Ⓕ	Ⓖ	Ⓗ	Ⓙ
41	Ⓐ	Ⓑ	Ⓒ	Ⓓ
42	Ⓕ	Ⓖ	Ⓗ	Ⓙ
43	Ⓐ	Ⓑ	Ⓒ	Ⓓ
44	Ⓕ	Ⓖ	Ⓗ	Ⓙ
45	Ⓐ	Ⓑ	Ⓒ	Ⓓ
46	Ⓕ	Ⓖ	Ⓗ	Ⓙ
47	Ⓐ	Ⓑ	Ⓒ	Ⓓ
48	Ⓕ	Ⓖ	Ⓗ	Ⓙ
49	Ⓐ	Ⓑ	Ⓒ	Ⓓ
50	Ⓕ	Ⓖ	Ⓗ	Ⓙ
51	Ⓐ	Ⓑ	Ⓒ	Ⓓ
52	Ⓕ	Ⓖ	Ⓗ	Ⓙ

Section 4: Math—Procedures

30 Minutes

30 Questions

Directions: *Make sure you have a watch to time yourself, a No. 2 pencil, and a ruler that has both metric and standard units. When you are ready, start timing yourself, and spend 30 minutes answering the questions in this section. Mark your answers on the answer sheet provided. If you are finished before the time is up, check over your work.*

Mathematics— Procedures

Directions

Read each question and select the best answer. Then mark the space for the answer you selected.

Sample

Maria developed 24 pictures of her birthday party and 36 pictures of her sister's wedding. How many pictures did she develop all together?

- (A) 50
- (B) 59
- (●) 60
- (D) 100
- (E) NH

1 $0.33 \times 212 =$

- (A) 0.6996
- (B) 6.998
- (C) 69.96
- (D) 69.98
- (E) NH

2 $3.1\overline{)93} =$

- (F) 3
- (G) 30
- (H) 33
- (J) 303
- (K) NH

3 Camp Cougar has 150 campers. 54% of the campers are boys. How many campers are boys?

- (A) 54
- (B) 69
- (C) 81
- (D) 96
- (E) NH

4 $108.1 \times 153.3 =$

- (F) 165.73
- (G) 1,671.73
- (H) 16,571.73
- (J) 165,711,73
- (K) NH

5 $7 \times 0.61 =$

- (A) 0.427
- (B) 4.27
- (C) 42.7
- (D) 427
- (E) NH

6 $6\frac{1}{4}$
      $+\,3\frac{3}{8}$

- (F) $9\frac{1}{2}$
- (G) $9\frac{5}{8}$
- (H) $10\frac{1}{4}$
- (J) $10\frac{1}{2}$
- (K) NH

GO ON

KAPLAN

7 $3\frac{1}{2}$
   $-\ 1\frac{3}{8}$

- Ⓐ $2\frac{3}{4}$
- Ⓑ $2\frac{1}{8}$
- Ⓒ $2\frac{1}{3}$
- Ⓓ $2\frac{1}{2}$
- Ⓔ   NH

8 Find 46% of 200.

- Ⓕ   46
- Ⓖ   92
- Ⓗ   920
- Ⓙ   9,200
- Ⓚ   NH

9 A rod of steel of $5\frac{7}{16}$ inches long. What is the the length rounded to the nearest half-inch?

- Ⓐ $7\frac{1}{2}$
- Ⓑ $5\frac{5}{8}$
- Ⓒ $5\frac{1}{4}$
- Ⓓ $5\frac{1}{2}$
- Ⓔ   NH

10 What is the number 186,592,578 when it is rounded to the nearest ten-thousands?

- Ⓕ   187,000,000
- Ⓖ   186,600,000
- Ⓗ   186,593,000
- Ⓙ   186,590,000
- Ⓚ   NH

11 At Riverdale High School, $\frac{4}{9}$ of the students are involved in some kind of athletic group. What is this fraction when rounded to the nearest percent?

- Ⓐ   4%
- Ⓑ   5%
- Ⓒ   40%
- Ⓓ   44%
- Ⓔ   NH

12 A quilt used $86\frac{4}{9}$ feet of fabric. What is that number rounded to the nearest whole number?

- Ⓕ   95
- Ⓖ   89
- Ⓗ   87
- Ⓙ   86
- Ⓚ   NH

GO ON

13 Phoebe charges $6.50 per hour to baby-sit. How many hours must she work to earn $136.50?

- (A) 1,36.5
- (B) 23
- (C) 22.5
- (D) 21
- (E) NH

14 Tom mowed $\frac{2}{3}$ of his lawn on Saturday and $\frac{1}{10}$ of it on Sunday.

What fraction of the lawn did Tom mow in the two days?

- (F) $\frac{23}{30}$
- (G) $\frac{3}{5}$
- (H) $\frac{20}{30}$
- (J) $\frac{3}{10}$
- (K) NH

15 In a pie-eating contest, Jack ate $4\frac{3}{4}$ pies and Tony ate $5\frac{3}{16}$ pies. How many pies did Jack and Tony eat together in total?

- (A) $10\frac{15}{16}$
- (B) $10\frac{1}{4}$
- (C) $9\frac{15}{16}$
- (D) $9\frac{1}{2}$
- (E) NH

16 To wrap a present, Melinda needs a ribbon that is $\frac{3}{5}$ foot long. She has a ribbon that is $\frac{7}{8}$ foot long.

$\frac{7}{8}$ of a foot

How much must Melinda cut off the ribbon to make it the correct length?

- (F) $\frac{1}{8}$ ft
- (G) $\frac{11}{40}$ ft
- (H) $\frac{23}{24}$ ft
- (J) $\frac{2}{5}$ ft
- (K) NH

17 Mandy has 30 boxes of pencils. Each box contains 25 pencils. How many pencils does Mandy have?

- (A) 250
- (B) 750
- (C) 2,500
- (D) 7,500
- (E) NH

GO ON

18 If tax is included in the prices, how much would a shirt, a pair of pants, a pair of shoes, and a belt cost all together?

$25.95
$39.50
$65.00
$19.99

Ⓕ $144.50
Ⓖ $150.44
Ⓗ $154.44
Ⓙ $160.94
Ⓚ NH

19 The Debate team held a pie sale and raised $228.

$3 each

What was the total number of pies sold?

Ⓐ 76
Ⓑ 96
Ⓒ 684
Ⓓ 704
Ⓔ NH

20 If tax is included in these prices, how much would skates, a helmet, and wrist guards cost all together?

skates $99.00
wrist guards $22.00
helmet $46.00

Ⓕ $87
Ⓖ $167
Ⓗ $176
Ⓙ $286
Ⓚ NH

21 There are 12 candy bars in each box. If 236 boxes are ordered, what is the total number of candy bars ordered?

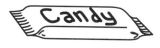

Candy

Ⓐ 2,832
Ⓑ 2,836
Ⓒ 28,342
Ⓓ 28,436
Ⓔ NH

GO ON

22 Sarah read $\frac{1}{8}$ of a book on Saturday and $\frac{6}{12}$ of it on Sunday. What fraction of her book had she read by Sunday?

- (F) $\frac{5}{8}$
- (G) $\frac{7}{8}$
- (H) $\frac{1}{2}$
- (J) $\frac{7}{20}$
- (K) NH

23 Alicia is selling some of the 768 coins in her collection. If she sells 34 coins on Monday, 65 coins on Tuesday and 193 coins during the rest of the week, how many coins will she have left?

- (A) 46
- (B) 466
- (C) 476
- (D) 506
- (E) NH

24 Ed has $9.00 for lunch. If he buys a hot dog for $2.48, cheese fries for $0.97 and a large soda for $1.08, how much money will he have left?

- (F) $0.47
- (G) $2.40
- (H) $4.40
- (J) $4.47
- (K) NH

25 Hamilton Middle School's girls' basketball team bought new uniforms for a total cost of $1,518. If there are 33 girls on the team, how much did each uniform cost?

- (A) $15
- (B) $46
- (C) $47
- (D) $330
- (E) NH

26 What would be the total cost of a T.V., V.C.R., and stereo if tax is included in these prices?

STEREO $385.57

T.V. $208.25

V.C.R. $146.92

- (F) $612.74
- (G) $740.74
- (H) $740.84
- (J) $1,700.84
- (K) NH

GO ON

27 375 students bought their lunch in the school cafeteria. If 52% of the students bought turkey sandwiches, how many students bought turkey sandwiches for lunch?

- (A) 52
- (B) 190
- (C) 195
- (D) 225
- (E) NH

28 Pablo bought 6 bags of these potato chips.

If each bag of potato chips contains $1\frac{1}{8}$ oz, how many ounces of potato chips did he buy in all?

- (F) $6\frac{3}{4}$
- (G) $6\frac{5}{8}$
- (H) $5\frac{7}{8}$
- (J) $4\frac{3}{4}$
- (K) NH

29 There are 37 Yum-Yum mini-doughnuts in one box. If the Fast-Mart orders 48 boxes, how many mini-doughnuts are they ordering?

- (A) 48
- (B) 1776
- (C) 1778
- (D) 17,786
- (E) NH

30 The middle-school field trip cost $7 per student. If the middle-school teachers collected a total of $4,123 for the trip, how many students paid for the trip?

- (F) 58
- (G) 59
- (H) 589
- (J) 599
- (K) NH

STOP

Answer Sheet

1 (A) (B) (C) (D) (E)

2 (F) (G) (H) (J) (K)

3 (A) (B) (C) (D) (E)

4 (F) (G) (H) (J) (K)

5 (A) (B) (C) (D) (E)

6 (F) (G) (H) (J) (K)

7 (A) (B) (C) (D) (E)

8 (F) (G) (H) (J) (K)

9 (A) (B) (C) (D) (E)

10 (F) (G) (H) (J) (K)

11 (A) (B) (C) (D) (E)

12 (F) (G) (H) (J) (K)

13 (A) (B) (C) (D) (E)

14 (F) (G) (H) (J) (K)

15 (A) (B) (C) (D) (E)

16 (F) (G) (H) (J) (K)

17 (A) (B) (C) (D) (E)

18 (F) (G) (H) (J) (K)

19 (A) (B) (C) (D) (E)

20 (F) (G) (H) (J) (K)

21 (A) (B) (C) (D) (E)

22 (F) (G) (H) (J) (K)

23 (A) (B) (C) (D) (E)

24 (F) (G) (H) (J) (K)

25 (A) (B) (C) (D) (E)

26 (F) (G) (H) (J) (K)

27 (A) (B) (C) (D) (E)

28 (F) (G) (H) (J) (K)

29 (A) (B) (C) (D) (E)

30 (F) (G) (H) (J) (K)

Section 5: Language

45 Minutes

48 Questions

Directions: *Make sure you have a watch to time yourself and a No. 2 pencil. When you are ready, start timing yourself, and spend 45 minutes answering the questions in this section. Mark your answers on the answer sheet provided. If you are finished before the time is up, check over your work.*

Language

Directions

Read each sentence, and focus on the underlined words. The sentence may contain an error in grammar, punctuation, or style. If you find a mistake, choose the answer that best corrects it. If you find no mistake, select *Correct as is.*

Sample

Their lack of fitness soon **become an issue** for the soccer team.

- ● became an issue
- Ⓑ become the issue
- Ⓒ become and issue
- Ⓓ Correct as is

---

1 When the team **have finished** running practice laps, we left the track.

- Ⓐ finished
- Ⓑ will have finish
- Ⓒ had finished
- Ⓓ Correct as is

2 With little **effort, the Teacher finished** the math problem in front of the whole class.

- Ⓕ effort the teacher finished
- Ⓖ effort, the teacher finished
- Ⓗ effort, the Teacher is finished
- Ⓙ Correct as is

3 She **would of gone to the dance if** Todd had asked her.

- Ⓐ would of gone to the dance had
- Ⓑ would have gone to the Dance if
- Ⓒ would have gone to the dance if
- Ⓓ Correct as is

4 The **Italian chefs** cooked a feast for the whole town.

- Ⓕ Italian chefs'
- Ⓖ Italian Chefs
- Ⓗ italian chef's
- Ⓙ Correct as is

5 Take the following items when **camping, a tent, a sleeping bag, and plenty of bug spray.**

- Ⓐ camping: a tent, a sleeping bag, and plenty of bug spray
- Ⓑ camping: a tent, a sleeping bag, and bring plenty of bug spray
- Ⓒ camping a tent, a sleeping bag, and plenty of bug spray
- Ⓓ Correct as is

6 As we sat by the pool, we drank soda and **ate brazilian food**.

- Ⓕ ate Brazilian food
- Ⓖ ate Brazilian Food
- Ⓗ eat brazilian food
- Ⓙ Correct as is

GO ON

7 If the restaurant had given <u>her and I a discount, we</u> would have returned there.

- (A) her and me a discount, we
- (B) her and I a discount we
- (C) her and me a discount we
- (D) Correct as is

8 One of the <u>runners are trying</u> to win the race by taking a shortcut.

- (F) runners' is trying
- (G) runners are tried
- (H) runners is trying
- (J) Correct as is

9 Doug said, "I am going to the park <u>this afternoon.</u>

- (A) this afternoon
- (B) this afternoon."
- (C) this Afternoon."
- (D) Correct as is

10 Our <u>Governor, Governor Moralis,</u> decided to lower our taxes this year.

- (F) Governor, Governor Moralis
- (G) governor, Governor Moralis,
- (H) Governor Governor Moralis
- (J) Correct as is

11 We are excited that our <u>team is now celebrating our</u> fifth anniversary.

- (A) team, is now celebrating its
- (B) team is now celebrating their
- (C) team is now celebrating its
- (D) Correct as is

12 My aunt lives on the <u>West Coast where its</u> sunny most of the time.

- (F) west coast where its
- (G) West Coast where it's
- (H) west coast where it's
- (J) Correct as is

13 The bird <u>flew quick over</u> the fenced yard.

- (A) flew quickly over
- (B) flew quicker, over
- (C) flew quickly, over
- (D) Correct as is

14 Michelle <u>demanded, Tell</u> me the truth about this book."

- (F) demanded, tell
- (G) demanded "Tell
- (H) demanded, "Tell
- (J) Correct as is

15 Monique knew that the <u>dragon, a friendly version of the monster</u> would help her find the treasure.

- (A) dragon a friendly version of the monster
- (B) dragon, a friendly, version of the monster,
- (C) dragon, a friendly version of the monster,
- (D) Correct as is

GO ON

16 After the party had ended, the DJ packed up her <u>speakers, records, and took her extra party favors</u>.

   F speakers, records, and extra party favors
   G speakers records and took her extra party favors
   H speakers, records, and took extra party favors
   J Correct as is

17 The families were thrilled that their pets would <u>live happy in the new kennel</u>.

   A live happily, in the new kennel
   B live happy in the new Kennel
   C live happily in the new kennel
   D Correct as is

18 Head <u>east to</u> get to the world's largest ball of yarn.

   F East to
   G east, to
   H East, to
   J Correct as is

19 Did you know that <u>doctor Lu is going</u> to receive an award next week?

   A Doctor Lu is going
   B Doctor Lu are going
   C doctor Lu, is going
   D Correct as is

20 Stravinsky's music caused a riot at <u>first and people</u> threw tomatoes at the orchestra.

   F first: people
   G first; people
   H first; People
   J Correct as is

21 As she entered the office, Rachel asked, "Hello, is anyone <u>there?</u>

   A there".
   B there
   C there?"
   D Correct as is

22 The Mississippi River, one of the longest in the United States, flows <u>South from its</u> origin.

   F south from its
   G South from it's
   H south from it's
   J Correct as is

23 All of the <u>students is going</u> to help with the fund drive.

   A student's are going
   B student's is going
   C students are going
   D Correct as is

24 The speaker today is <u>principal Moore, a</u> distinguished educator.

   F Principal Moore a
   G principal Moore a
   H Principal Moore, a
   J Correct as is

GO ON

Directions

Read the sentence(s) in the box. If there is an error in sentence structure or logic, select the choice that best corrects it. If the sentence contains no mistake, select *Correct as is*.

Sample

> **You are the person. That everyone wants to be president.**

- (A) You are the person. Which everyone want to be president.
- ● You are the person that everyone wants to be president.
- (C) You are the person everyone wants. To be president.
- (D) Correct as is

25

> **The audience clapped and applauded at the end of the concert.**

- (A) At the end of the concert, the audience clapped and applauded.
- (B) The audience applauded at the end of the concert.
- (C) Applauding, the audience clapped at the end of the concert.
- (D) Correct as is

26

> **Michael jumped through the air to catch the ball. And he caught it.**

- (F) Michael jumped through the air to catch the ball. And he caught the ball.
- (G) Michael jumped through the air to catch the ball, and he caught it.
- (H) Michael jumped through the air to catch it. He caught the ball.
- (J) Correct as is

27

> **Running and sprinting to get to the store on time, Louisa arrived just as they were locking the doors.**

- (A) Sprinting to get to the store on time, Louisa arrived just as they were locking the doors.
- (B) Louisa arrived just as they were locking the doors, sprinting and running.
- (C) Just as they were locking the doors, Louisa arrived sprinting and running.
- (D) Correct as is

28

> **I found the test to be hard. But fair.**

- (F) I found the test to be hard. And fair.
- (G) I found the test to be hard, but I found the test was also fair.
- (H) I found the test to be hard but fair.
- (J) Correct as is

GO ON

29 | Still in the refrigerator, I left my lunch at home.

- Ⓐ It, the lunch I left at home, was still in the refrigerator.
- Ⓑ I left my lunch in the refrigerator at home.
- Ⓒ Still in the refrigerator was the lunch that I left at home.
- Ⓓ Correct as is

30 | The moon has several small craters, in other places the craters are very deep.

- Ⓕ The moon has several small craters. In other places the craters are very deep.
- Ⓖ In other places the craters are very deep, and the moon has several small craters.
- Ⓗ The moon has several small craters. In other places. The craters are very deep.
- Ⓙ Correct as is

31 | The team visited the Hall of Fame they saw trophies and autographs.

- Ⓐ The team visited the Hall of Fame, they saw trophies and autographs.
- Ⓑ When the team visited the Hall of Fame, they saw trophies and autographs.
- Ⓒ The team, visiting the Hall of Fame and seeing trophies and autographs.
- Ⓓ Correct as is

32 | My sister cried and sobbed when the family cat died.

- Ⓕ Crying, my sister sobbed when the family cat died.
- Ⓖ My sister cried when the family cat died.
- Ⓗ My sister cried and she sobbed when the family cat died.
- Ⓙ Correct as is

GO ON

33

> Unwilling to surrender and the soldiers dove into the ditches.

- Ⓐ Unwilling to surrender, the soldiers dove into the ditches.
- Ⓑ Unwilling, to surrender and the soldiers dove into the ditches.
- Ⓒ The soldiers dove into the ditches and unwilling to surrender.
- Ⓓ Correct as is

34

> The captain could not see the shore and he had to use the radio and the ship came in late.

- Ⓕ The captain could not see the shore, he had to use the radio. The ship came in late.
- Ⓖ The captain, not able to see the shore, and the ship came in late.
- Ⓗ The captain could not see the shore. He had to use the radio, and the ship came in late.
- Ⓙ Correct as is

35

> Through the silky water, the dolphin swam like a slithery snake.

- Ⓐ Like a slithery snake, the dolphin swam through the silky water.
- Ⓑ The dolphin, it swam through the silky water like a slithery snake.
- Ⓒ Through the silky water, swam like a slithery snake the dolphin.
- Ⓓ Correct as is

36

> While talking on the phone, the cat got petted by Andre.

- Ⓕ While talking on the phone, Andre's cat got petted.
- Ⓖ While talking on the phone, Andre petted his cat.
- Ⓗ Andre petted his cat, while talking on the phone.
- Ⓙ Correct as is

GO ON

Paragraph Questions

Directions

Read the paragraph in the box. Then read the following questions. Select the best answer to each question based on the information in the paragraph.

Sample

Paragraph 1

Koala bears look like cuddly animals. Through photographs, the button noses and furry ears of the Koala make them popular with children everywhere. But visitors to Australia are often surprised to find out what Koalas are really like. Koalas often hiss and spit at people when they come near.

Which is the *main* reason this paragraph was written?

- ● to tell you about Koalas
- Ⓑ to describe the animals of Australia
- Ⓒ to compare different animals
- Ⓓ to make sure visitors to Australia are happy

GO ON

Paragraph 1

Did you ever ask yourself how flowers grow if they don't eat? Well, the truth is that they do eat. Flowers and other plants make their own food. It's as if they have little kitchens built into them. The flowers take sunlight, soil nutrients, and rain water to make a delicious combination of plant food. <u>If one of those ingredients is missing, the flower will not be able to eat. Eventually it will die.</u>

37 **Which of these would go *best* after the last sentence in this paragraph?**

    Ⓐ Sunlight is the most important ingredient in plant food.

    Ⓑ Fortunately, flowers are usually able to get all the ingredients to make their food.

    Ⓒ Depending on their size, some flowers make more food than others.

    Ⓓ People can help flowers make their food by giving them fertilizer.

38 **What would be the *best* way to begin the underlined sentence?**

    Ⓕ However,

    Ⓖ Therefore,

    Ⓗ Meanwhile,

    Ⓙ In any case,

GO ON

Paragraph 2

Robert had never been taught to sing or play the guitar. He just knew how to do it. Robert sang the blues to get rid of his sadness. Wherever Robert went, he found sadness. <u>He was always singing the blues.</u> His sadness fueled his music.

39 What is the *best* way to begin the underlined sentence?

- Ⓐ Because
- Ⓑ Meanwhile,
- Ⓒ Afterwards,
- Ⓓ Therefore,

40 Which of these would *not* belong in this paragraph?

- Ⓕ Robert decided to play guitar because of its sad sound.
- Ⓖ Robert had a mixture of talent, sadness, and desire to make blues music.
- Ⓗ Blues music developed into jazz in the early 1900s.
- Ⓙ The blues was Robert's favorite music because it allowed him to express himself.

Paragraph 3

Trevor sat high on the cliff of the mountain. He watched the glimmering water below. He breathed in the cool air and let the salt from the ocean settle on his tongue. Every day after his swim, Trevor made the long, strenuous climb up the side of the mountain. His spot on the edge of the cliff was marked by the patch of dirt where he always sat. This cliff over the ocean was where Trevor sat to think.

41 Which of these would *not* belong in this paragraph?

- Ⓐ Even in the rain, Trevor made his way up the mountainside to watch the sway of the ocean.

- Ⓑ The water below made Trevor think of the vast world that expanded before him.

- Ⓒ Mountains that are situated near the ocean are prone to landslides because their foundations are less stable.

- Ⓓ Trevor tried to keep his mind clear while he swam and climbed so that he could think better on the cliff.

GO ON

Paragraph 4

Dear David:

Congratulations on your perfect game last week. I think you are a truly great baseball player. Watching you achieve at that level made me proud to be a fan of yours.

I would like to set aside some time to talk to you in person next week. <u>Do you have time for lunch before your game on Thursday?</u> Congratulations again.

Sincerely yours,

George

---

42 **What is the _main_ purpose of this letter?**

- Ⓕ To request information
- Ⓖ To give praise
- Ⓗ To ask a question
- Ⓙ To make a complaint

43 **How can the first two sentences of this letter _best_ be combined?**

- Ⓐ Congratulations on your perfect game last week, I think you are a truly great baseball player.
- Ⓑ I think you are a truly great baseball player, congratulations on your perfect game last week.
- Ⓒ Congratulations on your perfect game last week; I think you are a truly great baseball player.
- Ⓓ A truly great baseball player, I would like to congratulate you on your perfect game last week

44 **What is the _best_ way to begin the underlined sentence?**

- Ⓕ So,
- Ⓖ However,
- Ⓗ For example,
- Ⓙ Finally,

45 **Which of these would _not_ belong in this letter?**

- Ⓐ You remind me of some of the amazing players who started this sport.
- Ⓑ Your game was one of the most exciting of the season.
- Ⓒ I think that you will have another perfect game sometime this year.
- Ⓓ Baseball is such a great sport that I would like to see it played in more countries.

46 **Which of these would go _best_ after the last sentence in this letter?**

- Ⓕ Best wishes from me and the rest of your fans.
- Ⓖ Maybe we can have lunch on Wednesday.
- Ⓗ Do you think we have a chance at the playoffs?
- Ⓙ What are your plans for the winter?

GO ON

Paragraph 5

Long ago, Egyptian kings were buried as mummies when they died. The kings did this as a gift to their gods. They also did this to display their wealth. The mummies were placed in fancy coffins that were covered with gold and colored glass. <u>The outside of the coffin had special words that told the history of the king buried inside.</u> The mummy ritual lasted for thousands of years in ancient Egypt.

47 **Which of these is the *best* topic sentence for this paragraph?**

    Ⓐ Mummies are in sacred burial grounds that should not be disturbed.

    Ⓑ Ancient Egyptian kings were buried as mummies in special coffins.

    Ⓒ Though the mummy ritual lasted a long time, they no longer do it.

    Ⓓ On Easter Island, the natives created giant statues for their gods.

48 **Which of these would *not* belong in this paragraph?**

    Ⓕ The mummy coffins also contained pictures dedicated to the gods.

    Ⓖ The kings wanted to display their wealth so they would be remembered forever.

    Ⓗ The mummy coffins were made out of expensive wood and other rare materials.

    Ⓘ On her last trip to Egypt, the President's wife visited the pyramids.

STOP

Answer Sheet

1	Ⓐ	Ⓑ	Ⓒ	Ⓓ		**25**	Ⓐ	Ⓑ	Ⓒ	Ⓓ
2	Ⓕ	Ⓖ	Ⓗ	Ⓙ		**26**	Ⓕ	Ⓖ	Ⓗ	Ⓙ
3	Ⓐ	Ⓑ	Ⓒ	Ⓓ		**27**	Ⓐ	Ⓑ	Ⓒ	Ⓓ
4	Ⓕ	Ⓖ	Ⓗ	Ⓙ		**28**	Ⓕ	Ⓖ	Ⓗ	Ⓙ
5	Ⓐ	Ⓑ	Ⓒ	Ⓓ		**29**	Ⓐ	Ⓑ	Ⓒ	Ⓓ
6	Ⓕ	Ⓖ	Ⓗ	Ⓙ		**30**	Ⓕ	Ⓖ	Ⓗ	Ⓙ
7	Ⓐ	Ⓑ	Ⓒ	Ⓓ		**31**	Ⓐ	Ⓑ	Ⓒ	Ⓓ
8	Ⓕ	Ⓖ	Ⓗ	Ⓙ		**32**	Ⓕ	Ⓖ	Ⓗ	Ⓙ
9	Ⓐ	Ⓑ	Ⓒ	Ⓓ		**33**	Ⓐ	Ⓑ	Ⓒ	Ⓓ
10	Ⓕ	Ⓖ	Ⓗ	Ⓙ		**34**	Ⓕ	Ⓖ	Ⓗ	Ⓙ
11	Ⓐ	Ⓑ	Ⓒ	Ⓓ		**35**	Ⓐ	Ⓑ	Ⓒ	Ⓓ
12	Ⓕ	Ⓖ	Ⓗ	Ⓙ		**36**	Ⓕ	Ⓖ	Ⓗ	Ⓙ
13	Ⓐ	Ⓑ	Ⓒ	Ⓓ		**37**	Ⓐ	Ⓑ	Ⓒ	Ⓓ
14	Ⓕ	Ⓖ	Ⓗ	Ⓙ		**38**	Ⓕ	Ⓖ	Ⓗ	Ⓙ
15	Ⓐ	Ⓑ	Ⓒ	Ⓓ		**39**	Ⓐ	Ⓑ	Ⓒ	Ⓓ
16	Ⓕ	Ⓖ	Ⓗ	Ⓙ		**40**	Ⓕ	Ⓖ	Ⓗ	Ⓙ
17	Ⓐ	Ⓑ	Ⓒ	Ⓓ		**41**	Ⓐ	Ⓑ	Ⓒ	Ⓓ
18	Ⓕ	Ⓖ	Ⓗ	Ⓙ		**42**	Ⓕ	Ⓖ	Ⓗ	Ⓙ
19	Ⓐ	Ⓑ	Ⓒ	Ⓓ		**43**	Ⓐ	Ⓑ	Ⓒ	Ⓓ
20	Ⓕ	Ⓖ	Ⓗ	Ⓙ		**44**	Ⓕ	Ⓖ	Ⓗ	Ⓙ
21	Ⓐ	Ⓑ	Ⓒ	Ⓓ		**45**	Ⓐ	Ⓑ	Ⓒ	Ⓓ
22	Ⓕ	Ⓖ	Ⓗ	Ⓙ		**46**	Ⓕ	Ⓖ	Ⓗ	Ⓙ
23	Ⓐ	Ⓑ	Ⓒ	Ⓓ		**47**	Ⓐ	Ⓑ	Ⓒ	Ⓓ
24	Ⓕ	Ⓖ	Ⓗ	Ⓙ		**48**	Ⓕ	Ⓖ	Ⓗ	Ⓙ

Section 6: Spelling

25 Minutes

30 Questions

Directions: *Make sure you have a watch to time yourself and a No. 2 pencil. When you are ready, start timing yourself, and spend 25 minutes answering the questions in this section. Mark your answers on the answer sheet provided. If you are finished before the time is up, check over your work.*

Spelling

Directions

If you see a word spelled incorrectly, mark it on your answer key. If no word is spelled incorrectly, select the "No mistake" answer choice.

Sample

- ● The wedding began <u>befour</u> noon.
- Ⓑ The depth of the water was hard to <u>measure</u>.
- Ⓒ My jacket was <u>stuck</u> in the door.
- Ⓓ No mistake

1 Ⓐ Please <u>close</u> the door behind you.
  Ⓑ I played well on the minature golf <u>course</u>.
  Ⓒ I wore a <u>plane</u> dress to the dance.
  Ⓓ No mistake

2 Ⓕ The weather <u>vane</u> pointed eastward.
  Ⓖ I can't wait until <u>it's</u> time for vacation.
  Ⓗ It was hard to <u>here</u> from where I was sitting.
  Ⓙ No mistake

3 Ⓐ I <u>knew</u> the answer to the question on the radio contest.
  Ⓑ I had a <u>hole</u> box of cough drops yesterday.
  Ⓒ When do you <u>need</u> to be picked up?
  Ⓓ No mistake

4 Ⓕ I want to <u>pare</u> the apple so it will cook more quickly.
  Ⓖ I ran up the <u>stares</u> to my room.
  Ⓗ I wasn't sure how much my pumpkin would <u>weigh</u>.
  Ⓙ No mistake

5 Ⓐ Did you choose the <u>write</u> answer for the last question?
  Ⓑ There was a big <u>knot</u> in my shoelace.
  Ⓒ My archaeologist uncle found an ancient Greek <u>urn</u>.
  Ⓓ No mistake

6 Ⓕ I can't <u>imagine</u> living anywhere else.
  Ⓖ I live right <u>buy</u> the park.
  Ⓗ There was not a <u>soul</u> in the house when I got home.
  Ⓙ No mistake

GO ON

7

Ⓐ There was a party to <u>celebrate</u> finishing the project.

Ⓑ What <u>department</u> does your mother work in?

Ⓒ It was important to pay <u>attencion</u> to the directions.

Ⓓ No mistake

8

Ⓕ Do you shop at that store <u>frequently</u>?

Ⓖ I try not to make a <u>habbit</u> of staying up late.

Ⓗ I had an <u>option</u> whether to go or not.

Ⓙ No mistake

9

Ⓐ That decision showed a real <u>errur</u> in judgement.

Ⓑ It's better to be <u>cautious</u> when you're in a new situation.

Ⓒ I looked at the bug under a <u>magnifying</u> glass.

Ⓓ No mistake

10

Ⓕ The room can <u>accommodate</u> 50 people.

Ⓖ I wonder how long it would take to count to one <u>billyun</u>.

Ⓗ I had to finish my paper before I could <u>graduate</u>.

Ⓙ No mistake

11

Ⓐ I made the directions as <u>simple</u> as possible.

Ⓑ Carla will <u>exchange</u> the shirt for one that fits.

Ⓒ He made a <u>ridiculous</u> suggestion just to be humorous.

Ⓓ No mistake

12

Ⓕ My favorite subject is <u>chemistrey</u>.

Ⓖ I picked out the cutest puppy from the <u>litter</u>.

Ⓗ I wanted a turkey <u>sandwich</u> for lunch.

Ⓙ No mistake

13

Ⓐ It's important to eat <u>protein</u> so you have plenty of energy.

Ⓑ The dancer moved very <u>gracefully</u>.

Ⓒ I knew I was in for a <u>lekture</u> when I talked back to my mother.

Ⓓ No mistake

14

Ⓕ You shouldn't believe every <u>roomor</u> you hear.

Ⓖ I wasn't sure who was going to <u>perform</u> that night.

Ⓗ It rained <u>extraordinarily</u> hard this morning.

Ⓙ No mistake

GO ON

15
- (A) My teacher has an <u>advanced</u> degree in English Literature.
- (B) I <u>tackled</u> that math problem and didn't stop until I got the answer.
- (C) I wanted to have my <u>fortun</u> told at the carnival.
- (D) No mistake

16
- (F) The movie <u>received</u> a good review.
- (G) He had <u>excellint</u> manners.
- (H) Cars go <u>extremely</u> fast on the highways.
- (J) No mistake

17
- (A) She wore a <u>mismatched</u> pair of socks.
- (B) I got a <u>generous</u> scholarship to college.
- (C) I find <u>multiplication</u> easy.
- (D) No mistake

18
- (F) The triangle had an <u>obtuse</u> angle.
- (G) The airplane took off without any <u>delaiys</u>.
- (H) I didn't find that movie <u>believable</u>.
- (J) No mistake

19
- (A) I have no <u>tolerance</u> for people who are rude.
- (B) I worked very hard on my job <u>appllication</u>.
- (C) Natori was amazed at the response of the <u>audience</u>.
- (D) No mistake

20
- (F) I tried to be very <u>patient</u> with the toddler.
- (G) I found the homework last night very <u>confuseing</u>.
- (H) The lion at the zoo let out a <u>fierce</u> roar.
- (J) No mistake

21
- (A) He was <u>motivated</u> to study because he could get an "A" for that year.
- (B) I like to know <u>exacttly</u> what I'm doing all the time.
- (C) He had a very strong <u>opinion</u> about the verdict.
- (D) No mistake

22
- (F) Bats, most active during the night, are <u>nocturnal</u> creatures.
- (G) The <u>mountain</u> loomed large in the distance.
- (H) She had a very <u>intelligent</u> response to the question.
- (J) No mistake

GO ON

23
  (A) I was <u>distracted</u> by the noise of the sirens.
  (B) <u>Fortunately</u>, she had an extra set of keys to use.
  (C) She has a <u>remarkkable</u> talent for soccer.
  (D) No mistake

24
  (F) It was a <u>casual</u> meeting of friends.
  (G) The invitation said "<u>festtive</u> attire."
  (H) I <u>completed</u> the exam with time to spare.
  (J) No mistake

25
  (A) Baking cookies turned into a <u>collasal</u> mess.
  (B) I was <u>grateful</u> for the long weekend.
  (C) He was a <u>successful</u> politician.
  (D) No mistake

26
  (F) Dress <u>reahearsal</u> is Thursday.
  (G) What are your job <u>qualifications</u>?
  (H) Jonas made an <u>angular</u> movement with his arms.
  (J) No mistake

27
  (A) The <u>statistishan</u> was named Robert.
  (B) The truck could not stop it <u>momentum</u>.
  (C) I need your <u>input</u>.
  (D) No mistake

28
  (F) <u>Furthermore</u>, I need more time.
  (G) <u>Neptune</u> is a cold planet.
  (H) The coach <u>desputed</u> the call.
  (J) No mistake

29
  (A) Are these readings <u>accurate</u>?
  (B) We <u>congradulated</u> the winner.
  (C) Take these <u>wrappings</u> away.
  (D) No mistake

30
  (F) That is a <u>drastic</u> action.
  (G) The boss <u>instituted</u> the new program.
  (H) The house <u>appraisel</u> was fair.
  (J) No mistake

STOP

Answer Sheet

1	(A)	(B)	(C)	(D)	16	(F)	(G)	(H)	(J)
2	(F)	(G)	(H)	(J)	17	(A)	(B)	(C)	(D)
3	(A)	(B)	(C)	(D)	18	(F)	(G)	(H)	(J)
4	(F)	(G)	(H)	(J)	19	(A)	(B)	(C)	(D)
5	(A)	(B)	(C)	(D)	20	(F)	(G)	(H)	(J)
6	(F)	(G)	(H)	(J)	21	(A)	(B)	(C)	(D)
7	(A)	(B)	(C)	(D)	22	(F)	(G)	(H)	(J)
8	(F)	(G)	(H)	(J)	23	(A)	(B)	(C)	(D)
9	(A)	(B)	(C)	(D)	24	(F)	(G)	(H)	(J)
10	(F)	(G)	(H)	(J)	25	(A)	(B)	(C)	(D)
11	(A)	(B)	(C)	(D)	26	(F)	(G)	(H)	(J)
12	(F)	(G)	(H)	(J)	27	(A)	(B)	(C)	(D)
13	(A)	(B)	(C)	(D)	28	(F)	(G)	(H)	(J)
14	(F)	(G)	(H)	(J)	29	(A)	(B)	(C)	(D)
15	(A)	(B)	(C)	(D)	30	(F)	(G)	(H)	(J)

PRACTICE TEST A

Answer Key

Reading Vocabulary

1	C
2	F
3	B
4	J
5	A
6	H
7	C
8	F
9	B
10	H
11	A
12	H
13	C
14	G
15	C
16	H
17	C
18	H
19	A
20	F
21	A
22	H
23	B
24	G
25	D
26	H
27	B
28	J
29	A
30	H

Reading Comprehension

1	D	28	H
2	G	29	C
3	A	30	H
4	J	31	C
5	C	32	H
6	F	33	B
7	C	34	F
8	G	35	C
9	C	36	F
10	F	37	D
11	C	38	H
12	J	39	D
13	D	40	G
14	F	41	B
15	A	42	H
16	F	43	B
17	B	44	J
18	J	45	C
19	B	46	G
20	F	47	C
21	C	48	J
22	G	49	C
23	D	50	F
24	H	51	C
25	A	52	J
26	G	53	A
27	D	54	G

Mathematics—Problem Solving

1	A	27	D
2	G	28	G
3	D	29	B
4	H	30	F
5	D	31	C
6	G	32	J
7	B	33	C
8	G	34	H
9	C	35	B
10	J	36	H
11	B	37	B
12	H	38	G
13	B	39	C
14	G	40	G
15	C	41	B
16	H	42	H
17	C	43	A
18	G	44	G
19	C	45	D
20	J	46	J
21	C	47	A
22	J	48	H
23	C	49	B
24	G	50	J
25	C	51	C
26	H	52	F

Mathematics—Procedures

1	C
2	G
3	C
4	H
5	B
6	G
7	B
8	G
9	C
10	J
11	D
12	J
13	D
14	F
15	C
16	G
17	B
18	G
19	A
20	G
21	A
22	F
23	C
24	J
25	B
26	G
27	C
28	F
29	B
30	H

Language

1	A	25	B
2	G	26	G
3	C	27	A
4	J	28	H
5	A	29	B
6	F	30	F
7	A	31	B
8	H	32	G
9	B	33	A
10	G	34	H
11	C	35	A
12	G	36	G
13	A	37	B
14	H	38	F
15	C	39	D
16	F	40	H
17	C	41	C
18	J	42	G
19	A	43	C
20	G	44	F
21	C	45	D
22	F	46	F
23	C	47	B
24	H	48	J

Spelling

1	C
2	H
3	B
4	G
5	A
6	G
7	C
8	G
9	A
10	G
11	D
12	F
13	C
14	F
15	C
16	G
17	D
18	G
19	B
20	G
21	B
22	J
23	C
24	G
25	A
26	F
27	A
28	H
29	B
30	H

Answers and Explanations for Practice Test A

Answers and Explanations for Practice Test A

 ## READING VOCABULARY

Questions 1–16: Synonyms

Just over half of the Reading Vocabulary section consists of Synonym questions, so performing well in this area is important. The underlined words are usually nouns or verbs, but expect 1–3 adjectives or adverbs as well.

While it would be useful to know the each of the words in question outright, you should not be discouraged if this is not the case. When faced with an unknown word, remember this key fact:

You do not need to know the exact dictionary definition of a word. If you have a general idea of its definition, that should be enough to help you eliminate some answer choices and guess.

Sometimes, thinking in terms of *positive/negative* can lead to the correct answer. For instance, if you don't exactly know what the word *commend* means, but you know that it means something positive, then you can go to the answer choices and eliminate any negative answer choices, since there's no way a positive word will have a negative synonym. (The reverse is also true, of course.)

Question 1   Choice **D** sounds very similar to *contract*, but similar-sounding words are almost always incorrect answer choices, so it should be eliminated. Choice **A**, *lengthen*, is actually the antonym of *contract*. The answer is **C**.

Question 2   *Positive/negative* can be useful here. The *de-* in *depress* should lead you to think the word is negative, which allows you to cross out positive answer choices like **G**, **H**, and **J**. This leaves **F** as the only possible answer.

Question 3   Again, *grave* should make you think of a negative word (a *grave* where a person is buried is not a positive place), which allows you to cross out **A** and **C**. **B** is correct.

Question 4   *Converse* is the root of the more common word *conversation*, and a conversation is where two or more people *discuss* something. The answer is **J**.

Question 5   **A** is correct. The fact that there is very little in terms of technique to use on this problem illustrates how an expansive vocabulary is the best tool for this test section.

Question 6   Similar to question 4, the word *declare* in question 6 is the root of the better-known word *declaration*. *Declaration* is better known because of the famous Declaration of Independence, in which the U.S. *announced* its freedom. **H**.

Question 7   *Doubt* is a negative word, but unfortunately all the answer choices are also negative, so none can be crossed out. **C** is the best response.

Question 8   *Mainly* is an adverb, and this question might be approached in a simpler direction by eliminating all the *-ly's*. This gives you *main*, and the best synonym for this is *chief*, choice **F**.

Question 9   Many teenagers often complain of having parents who are too *strict*. **B** and **C** are both viable choices, but **B** is the correct response.

Question 10   The answer is **H**.

Question 11   Students who are having trouble in a particular subject sometimes get another student to *tutor*, or *teach*, them in that subject. **A**.

Question 12   This word is most often associated with illness, and while the answer choices are all negative, the best response is **H**, *disease*. *Wound*, *injury*, and *accident* imply acute rather than long-term conditions; cancer is usually a chronic condition.

Question 13   *Luxurious*, which may remind you of the word *luxury*, is therefore a positive word. Choice **A** can be crossed out. The answer is **C**.

Question 14   This is a positive word, so **J** and also **F** can be crossed out. Out of the two remaining choices, **G** is correct.

Question 15   The answer is **C**.

Question 16   *Vilify* is a negative word, allowing **F** and **G** to be eliminated. Of the two remaining choices, *analyze* is not very positive or negative—if anything, some would argue that it is a positive word—which leaves **H**.

Questions 17–23: Multiple Meaning Questions

Correctly determining the part of speech of the underlined word in the boxed sentence is a good technique on these questions. For example, if you determine that the underlined word in the boxed sentence is used as a noun, you can eliminate any answer choices that use the underlined word as a verb or adjective. This should leave with 1–3 choices left to choose from, greatly increasing your odds of answering the questions correctly.

Question 17   If you realize that *current* is used as a noun, you can then cross out choices **A**, **B** and **D** since they use *current* as an adjective. **C**.

Question 18   *Medium* is used as an adjective, which allows you to cross out **F** and **G**. **H** is correct, as *medium* is used to denote size.

Question 19   In this case, *store* is used as a verb, so **A** must be correct, as the other choices use *store* as a noun.

Question 20   *Bear* is a verb in the boxed sentence, so **G** and **J** are not going to be the answer. **F** is correct.

Question 21   *Conduct* is a verb in the boxed sentence, but only **D** can be crossed off. Since *conduct* means *behave* in the boxed sentence, **A** is the best choice.

Question 22   Since *spot* is a verb, nouns **F** and **G** will not be correct. **H**.

Question 23   *Court* is a noun, so choices **A** and **D** (which are verbs) can be eliminated. The boxed sentence refers to a *court of law*, so **B** is the answer.

Questions 24–30: Vocabulary–in–Context

Questions 24–30 are called Context questions since the key to understanding the underlined word hinges upon whether or not you can correctly determine how that specific word fits in with the meaning, or context, of the entire sentence. Therefore, the approach to these questions is straightforward: Read the sentence and use clues within the sentence to determine the definition of the underlined word. Next, go to the answer choices and find the word that is closest to the definition you came up with.

Question 24   A key clue is *finally*, showing that the conclusion comes at the *ending* of the movie. **G.**

Question 25   *Directions* normally tell you how to operate a machine, and what the *purpose* of items are. The answer is **D**.

Question 26   The phrase *no one else would think of* leads to choice **H**, *distinctive*.

Question 27   The meaning of the sentence is that one person created the product in their head, while the other person actually made the product. The best translation of *created the product in their head* is *idea*, choice **B**.

Question 28   **G** is incorrect because the phrase *small majority* makes little sense. **J** works best, since someone whose stomach hurts would only want a small amount, or *part*, of a meal. Notice that the sound-alikes *potion* and *partition* are both wrong.

Question 29   Since pennies are being used instead of checkers, the pennies have *replaced* the checkers. **A**

Question 30   *When they won* is positive, **F**, **G** and even **J** are not good choices. This leaves only **H**.

READING COMPREHENSION

The best approach to Reading Comprehension passages is to read the passage through the first time in order to understand the main point, and then head to the questions but **constantly refer** to the passage in order to make sure you have the correct answer. Many students attempt to answer the questions from memory, since they feel this saves time on the section. While it may shave off some seconds, it also leads to incorrect responses. Since the passage is always available, it is crucial that it be used in order to find the best answer choice.

Question 1   As the question asks how much *you will pay*, the best place to look for the answer is next to *Ticket Prices*. The third column, *Three or more days*, shows a price of $22 for a family. **D**.

Question 2   **G** makes the most sense, since this is an event with *local artists, musicians, and crafters* presenting *to the entire community* (first paragraph).

Question 3   Choices **C** and **D** can be found in the first paragraph; choice **B** is mentioned in the paragraph next to *October 12*. This leaves only **A**. Also, note that questions 2 and 3 were both solved using the same facts from the passage, although the questions themselves were very different.

Question 4   The phrase *Community Orchestra* can be found next to *October 12*, so **J** is the answer.

Question 5   The first word of the flyer is *Annual*, and it is repeated in the first sentence of the first paragraph below. This would lead to choice **C**.

Question 6   On this question, since *Main Lawn* is mentioned, it may be easier to go to that section of the passage and then use process of elimination. Looking at the entries across from *Main Lawn*, choices **G**, **H**, and **J** can be found and eliminated. **F** is the answer.

Question 7   **C** is the answer, and it draws on the same information as question 2.

Question 8   **F** is not stated anywhere, and **H** and **J** could be true but don't have to be. Only **G** can be proved with the information directly on the flyer.

Question 9   The first paragraph starts with Jeremy in the kitchen listening to the clock strike five times, so **C** is the answer.

Question 10   The main idea of this story is that Jeremy, who usually needs help from Ben, now must help Ben in his studying. **F** is correct.

Question 11   Since his brother received an A and thanked him, Jeremy feels glad, **C**.

Question 12   The end of the fourth paragraph states that Jeremy was *still behind in his schoolwork*. **J**.

Question 13   The use of the first person, and the fact that the events described were of a personal nature, makes **D** the best choice.

Question 14   The first sentence of the seventh paragraph states *Yesterday, Ben took the test*. **F**.

Question 15   Ben initially looks and acts serious, but he received an **A**. He was simply fooling his little brother, choice **A**.

Question 16   On questions dealing with emotions, positive responses are often correct, since the characters in the passages are rarely mean or bad-tempered. The answer in this case is **F**, *honored*.

Question 17   **B** is the answer since it deals with "Entry Into Art Colleges."

Question 18   **J** is the answer, as the bibliographical text states that it was found online.

Question 19   **A**, **C**, and **D**, all discuss creating art from objects already owned or easily found. This leaves **B** as the only choice.

Question 20   Paul Louiz wrote an article about "Make Your Own Paper," so he is probably the best informed about this process. **F**.

Question 21   **C** is correct.

Question 22   The function of a power station is to generate electrical current, **G**. Also, the second-to-last paragraph implies that everything else—such as bulbs and cable—was already in place, and all that was needed was current.

Question 23   From the last two lines of the passage, people were shouting in amazement as the office buildings lit up. **D**.

Question 24 The main idea of this passage revolves around Edison and his efforts with electricity. **H** is the best answer.

Question 25 The phrase it would *make him a rich man* should lead you to **A**.

Question 26 Again, since the main idea is about Edison, **G** is the best choice. This question, along with question 24, illustrates how knowing the main idea is crucial for understanding the passage and answering questions about it.

Question 27 Paragraph 7 discusses Edison's breakthrough using simple cotton thread. **D**.

Question 28 Since the paragraph states that other inventors had also worked to invent the light bulb, choice **H** is the best answer.

Question 29 **C** is the best answer, since the passage ends with the first introduction of electricity. A logical way to continue would be to talk about what happened afterwards.

Question 30 The answer to this question can be found in the middle of the first paragraph. **H**.

Question 31 Since meadow animals had been disappearing, Rabbit thought that Bear might have been eating them. This is why Rabbit jumped into the river in the first place. However, when Bear jumped into the river, it was to save Rabbit. This is opposite of what Rabbit thought, which is why Rabbit was confused and terrified. **C**.

Question 32 **H** is correct, since the second paragraph shows that the water was too fast for Rabbit.

Question 33 Two kid's events take place under the willow tree. **B**.

Question 34 Choice **J** is a trap because it shows what the adults will be doing at 1 P.M. The correct answer is **F**.

Question 35 There are two ways to answer this question. The first is to notice the small print underneath the *Where* at the top that excludes *Pointe Green*, choice **C**. The other method is simply process of elimination.

Question 36 **F** is the answer.

Question 37 Choice **B** is a trap since that is what adults will be doing at 1 P.M., but at 2:30 the correct answer is **D**.

Question 38 Across from the word *Cost* near the top of the passage is the answer, which is a *can of food* is needed for entry. **H**.

Question 39 *Mr. Cool* is performing on the baseball field; fans usually watch baseball games from long rows of benches known as *bleachers*, so **D** is the best choice.

Question 40 **G** is correct, since across from *When* is the reminder *One Day Only!*

The following questions come after two consecutive passages. This makes your task a little more difficult, as you must first decide which passage contains the information needed to answer each question. However, once this task is accomplished, the questions can be treated like any other Reading Comprehension problems.

Question 41 Attaching the bait is listed as the second step, and the third step is to *cast your line*. **B**.

Question 42 **H** is correct, as the description of the bisque refers to it as a soup later.

Question 43 The small print at the bottom of Kay's page mentions "cash only." **B**.

Question 44 Choices **F**, **G**, and **H** are all listed under *Materials You Will Need*, leaving **J**.

Question 45 Since fishing is a sport, the best choices are either **B** or **C**. There's little historical value to the passage, however, so **C** is the better choice.

Question 46 The first sentence states that Tumbleweed was found in a barn. This would lead one to answer **G**, *a farm*.

Question 47 The second line of the first paragraph explain how the mouse was "so young that his eyes were still closed." **C**.

Question 48 From the third sentence in the second paragraph, you learn that the absence of Tumbleweed's mother would be the most likely explanation for his demise. **J**.

Question 49 Both **B** and **C** have the key word in them—*animal*—but **C** discusses the *development*, or growth, of animals, so it is the better choice.

Question 50   The third paragraph contains the key clue for this question, the fact that Tumbleweed's eyes were open. **F.**

Question 51   While articles are placed in quotation marks, books are shown *italicized*. **C.**

Question 52   **J** is the answer, as Ms. Killburn wrote the article "Why Children Like Music."

Question 53   Since a dictionary provides explanations for unknown words or terms, **A** is the best choice.

Question 54   **G** is correct.

MATHEMATICS—PROBLEM SOLVING

This is the first of two Math sections (Math—Procedures is the other one). In Problem Solving, almost all of the questions require you to do some reading, so be prepared to answer some multistep problems that may take 2–3 minutes to work on. Bear in mind that since there is no guessing penalty on any part of the STAR tests, you should always answer every question, even if you are unsure of the problem. If possible, use process of elimination to get rid of unlikely answer choices, and then take an educated guess.

Questions 1–6: Number Sense and Numeration

These six questions deal with basic math concepts such as number lines, ordering numbers from least to greatest, and expanded notation. A sound background in basic math principles is the best tool to succeed on these questions.

Question 1   Since all of Margaret's actions were purchases of some form or another, the total cost will be $45.91 + $6 + $12.35 = $64.26, choice **A.**

Question 2   The fact that Javier has $900 is irrelevant, as it has nothing to do with what the actual question is. Some questions will have unnecessary information in order to confuse a student. To solve this problem, multiply the number of nights Javier is staying (4) with the cost per night ($78). 4 × 78 = $312, choice **G.**

Question 3   100 − 19 = 81 points. **D.**

Question 4   This question is a little different because it is using time. Some students may think $2\frac{1}{2}$ hours is 2 hours, 50 minutes, since 50 is half of a hundred (these students would pick **J**). However, the correct amount of time is 2 hours, 30 minutes, since there are 60 minutes in an hour. 7:55 + 2 hours , 30 minutes = 10:25 P.M. **H.**

Question 5   It helps to write out each part of the formula so that you do not make a careless error.

$V = l \times w \times h$

$V = 8 \times 3 \times 4$

$V = 96$ cubic inches, choice **D.**

Question 6   The cost of a hamburger and fries together is $1.75 + $0.85 = $2.60, and since three people (Joey, Derek, and Shelley) each had this order, the total cost is $2.60 × 3 people = $7.80, choice **G.**

Questions 7–10: Number Systems and Number Theory

The four questions in this category test a student's knowledge of such math concepts as prime numbers, scientific notation, as well as the basic facts underlying addition, subtraction, multiplication, and division.

Question 7   To find how much more money he earned in 1999, subtract 1997 earnings from 1999 earnings. $205.75 − $100.50 = $105.25, choice **B.**

Question 8   The 4 is in the hundredths spot. **G.**

Question 9   This question looks confusing at first, but if you can shake off the initial strangeness, the answer is fairly straightforward. The key indicates that every block equals 0.1. In this case, simply add up the number of blocks and then multiply that number by 0.1. There are 233 blocks, so 233 × 0.1 = 23.3, **C.**

Question 10   In scientific notation, the superscript number after the 10—in this case, 7— shows the number of decimal places that must be moved to the right. $9.30 \times 10^7 = 93{,}000{,}000$, choice **J.**

Questions 11–15 : Algebra

Algebra questions center around basic algebraic concepts such as solving linear equations, and finding the numeric value of variables.

Question 11 To solve this linear equation, place a 3 where the x appears

$Y = x^2$

$Y = 3^2$

$Y = 9$, choice **B**.

Question 12 Like the previous problem, the key to algebra questions is to write out the linear equation with the variables first, and then substitute the numeric values given in the question.

$P = 2l + 2w$

$P = 2(3) + 2(1)$

$P = 6 + 2$

$P = 8$, choice **H**.

Question 13 $T = 0.25m + 5$

$T = 0.25(40) + 5$

$T = 10 + 5$

$T = 15$, choice **B**.

Question 14 $R = \frac{d}{t}$

$R = \frac{12 \text{ kilometers}}{2 \text{ hours}}$

$R = 6$ km/hr, choice **G**.

Question 15 $V = 3g + 2$

$V = 3(4) + 2$

$V = 12 + 2$

$V = 14$, choice **C**.

Questions 16–18: Patterns and Functions

As its name suggests, the three questions here test a student's ability to recognize and manipulate visual or mathematical patterns.

Question 16   A glance at the numbers above 500 should reveal that the numbers on the right side are always 3 greater than the number on the left side. Since the number machine adds 3 each time, the number opposite 500 will be 503. **H.**

Question 17   There are two ways to answer this question. The first is to find the typist's rate per minute: $\frac{2 \text{ pages}}{5 \text{ minutes}} = 1$ page every 2.5 minutes. Therefore, for 100 pages of text, it would take 100×2.5 minutes = 250 minutes, or 4 hours, 10 minutes. Remember that there are 60 minutes in an hour, so this number equals $4\frac{10}{60}$, or $4\frac{1}{6}$, choice **C.** The other method would be to realize that $\left[\frac{2 \text{ pages}}{5 \text{ minutes}}\right] \times 50 = 100$ pages in 250 minutes. The rest of the math is then similar.

Question 18   The key to this problem is recognizing that each level of cans is a perfect square. The first level is $3 \times 3 = 9$, then next level is $4 \times 4 = 16$, and so on.

Going from top to bottom, then, the answer is $9 + 16 + 25 + 36 + 49 = 135$, choice **G.** Choice **J** could also be eliminated for being too large.

Questions 19–27: Statistics and Probability

These questions usually involve a chart or graph of some form. Gaining familiarity with the different kind of charts and graphs, such as pie charts and line graphs, is the key factor to doing well on these questions.

Question 19   Since *mean* is another word for average, to find Kathy's average travel time you must add up all the times and then divide by the number of days, 5.

$\frac{22.3 + 19.6 + 25.7 + 28.2 + 23.9}{5 \text{ days}} = \frac{119.7}{5} = 23.94$, choice **C.**

Question 20   In a set of numbers, the number that appears the most times is called the *mode*. In the long jump results, the number that appears the most times (twice) is 12 feet, 5 inches. **J.**

Question 21   Five out of a 100 people is a rather small amount (only 1 out of 20), so the best answer is pineapple. **C.**

Question 22 On coordinate problems, the numbers are always listed as (horizontal value, vertical value). Since the upper right hand corner is 4 spaces to the right of 0 and 5 spaces above it, the answer is (4, 5). **J.**

Question 23 Similar to the problem above, the answer here is (2, 4). **C.**

Question 24 Baymore was at $50 in April, while Amcor was at $25, so the difference in price is $50 − $25 = $25. **G.**

Question 25 Argville crossed 12,000 in about 1973, while Danton did not reach that level until 1990. 1990 − 1973 = 17 years, so the closest answer is **C** (notice the question says "*about* how much").

Question 26 The discount on all the other tickets is between $14 and $16 every time, so you should look for an answer choice around $87 − $14 = $73. **H** is the best choice.

Question 27 Looking at the numbers for Los Angeles and Oakland, you will see that the three-day rental is always twice as much as the one-day rental. If a one-day rental in Aspen is $78, then the three-day rental must be $78 × 2 = $156, answer **D.**

Questions 28–36: Geometry

Geometry questions primarily cover problems involving two- and three-dimensional geometric shapes like squares, triangles, trapezoids, and circles. In addition, there is also an occasional questions involving coordinates, symmetry, or rotation.

Question 28 **G** is correct, as all trapezoids have two obtuse and two acute angles, and no right angles.

Question 29 $V = l \times w \times h$

$V = 3 \times 2 \times 1$

$V = 6$ cubic feet, **B.**

Question 30 A line extending from the center of a circle to its edge is the definition of a radius. **F.**

Question 31   This question is really asking for the circumference of a circle with a diameter of 20 inches. Since the formula for circumference is C= πd, and you can approximate π = 3.14, then the answer is C = 3.14 $\times$ 20 = 62.8. **C.**

Question 32   The answer is **J**, parallel lines.

Question 33   The definition of an octagon is a figure with eight sides. **C.**

Question 34 $V = l \times w \times h$

$V = 20 \times 20 \times 12$

$V = 4,800$ cubic inches, **H.**

Question 35   Since the area of an object measures the space inside the figure, your eye should be drawn to choice **B** as the figure with the smallest area.

Question 36   Using the formula for the area of a triangle that is provided,

$A = \frac{1}{2} \times b \times h$

$A = \frac{1}{2} \times 5 \times 3$

$A = 7.5$ square feet, choice **H.**

Questions 37–41: Measurement

Many of these questions simply require a student to use a ruler and measure a figure correctly. Other Measurement questions include counting change, comparing lengths, using the appropriate units (meters instead of gallons, for example), or reading a scientific instrument, such as a barometer, correctly.

Question 37   Adding ten degrees to −10 degrees will place the temperature at zero degrees Celsius. **B.**

Question 38   The arrow is located between the 5 and 6 on the side of the swimming pool, so choices **H** and **J** can be eliminated. This leaves **F** and **G**, and since the arrow is past the halfway point, **G** is the closest.

Question 39   100 − 14 = 86 points. **C.**

KAPLAN

Question 40   **J** can be eliminated since it is a positive (high tide) number, and **F** is incorrect since the -3 is not even showing. Since the water line is halfway down from -2, **G** is the better choice.

Question 41 $-13 + 43 = 30$ degrees Fahrenheit. **B**.

Question 42–47: Estimation

As the name suggests, Estimation problems require students to round off numbers properly to find the right estimate.

Question 42   A six is in the thousandths place, and a 3 is in the ten-thousandths place, so 0.676 is correct. **H**.

Question 43 $\frac{7}{16}$ is a little less then half, so $144\frac{7}{16}$ is closer to 144 than 145. **A**.

Question 44   Thinking in terms of decimals makes this problem easier. Quarter-miles units would be: 3, 3.25, 3.50, 3.75, and so on. The fraction $3\frac{1}{3}$ would be converted to 3.33, and this is closer to 3.25 (0.08 difference) than it is to 3.50 (0.17 difference). Or you can use common denominators to arrive at $3\frac{4}{12}$, which is closest to answer **G**.

Question 45   73% is very close to 75%, and since $75\% = \frac{75}{100} = \frac{3}{4}$, the answer is **D**. (Remember that "percent" means "out of 100").

Question 46   The fish is just around the 7 inch mark, so **J** is the best response.

Question 47   Randy has about an 88, while Patrick has a 76, so $88 - 76 = 12$. The closest answer is choice **A**.

Questions 48–52: Problem Solving Strategies

This broad category covers a variety of different question types, but mostly these problems test whether or nor a student understands the steps needed to answer a particular question properly.

Question 48   In addition to the end time, you need the start time in order to find the length of the nap. **H.**

Question 49   Process of elimination (POE) is effective on this multistep problem. The first clue, that writing or spelling is never first, gets rids of **C**. The second clue eliminates **A** and **D**, leaving only **B**.

Question 50   **J** is the answer.

Question 51   On this question, the first clue gets rids of **A** and **B** The second clue does nothing to either **C** or **D**, but the third clue eliminates **D**. **C** is the answer.

Question 52   The first clue listed eliminates **G**, **H**, and **J**, leaving only **F**.

MATHEMATICS: PROCEDURES

About one-fourth of the questions in this section are straightforward numerical math problems. A key to answering these questions correctly is to write all your work down, as attempting to answer these questions in your head often leads to careless errors. These need to be avoided at all cost, as careless errors are a useless waste of points.

There are five possible answer choices on this section, as opposed to the usual four. The fifth choice is always *NH*, which stands for *Not Here*. If you work a problem and then do not find the answer in the first four choices, rework the problem. If you get the same answer the second time, pick NH and move on to the next question.

Question 1   **C.**

Question 2   **G.**

Question 3   **C.**

Question 4   **H.**

Question 5   B.

Question 6   In order to add fractions, you need to have a common denominator. On this question, multiplying $\frac{1}{4}$ by 2 yields $\frac{2}{8}$, so now both fractions have the common denominator of 8. **G** is the answer.

Question 7   B.

Question 8   G.

Questions 9–12: Rounding

These questions are similar to the Estimation questions in the Math—Problem Solving section.

Question 9 $\frac{7}{16}$ is just slightly less than half, so the length would be $5\frac{1}{2}$ inches, **C**.

Question 10   There is a 9 in the ten-thousands place, and a 2 in the thousands place, so the rounded number should be 186,590,000. **J**.

Question 11   The answer is 0.4444 with the fours repeating infinitely; the percent would be 44%. **D**.

Question 12   86 is the nearest whole number, since $\frac{4}{9}$ is less than half. **J**.

Questions 13–30: Computation-in-Context

These questions are primarily word problems. The key is to read the text carefully, and then decide what math operation—addition, subtraction, multiplication, or division—needs to be performed to get the correct answer.

Question 13   To find the number of hours needed, you will have to divide the total amount, $136.50, by Phoebe's hourly rate of $6.50. $\frac{136.5}{6.5} = 21$ hours, choice **D**.

Question 14   The key is to convert both fractions so that they have a common denominator of 30. $\frac{2}{3} \times 10 = \frac{20}{30}$ and $\frac{1}{10} \times 3 = \frac{3}{30}$. $\frac{20}{30} + \frac{3}{30} = \frac{23}{30}$. **F**.

Question 15 $\frac{3}{4} \times 4 = \frac{12}{16}$. Adding the two numbers together now, you get $4\frac{12}{16} + 5\frac{3}{16} = 9\frac{15}{16}$, choice **C**.

Question 16 $\frac{3}{5} \times 8 = \frac{24}{40}$ and $\frac{7}{8} \times 5 = \frac{35}{40}$. To find the length she needs to cut off, subtract the two numbers: $\frac{35}{40} - \frac{24}{40} = \frac{11}{40}$, choice **G**.

Question 17   To find the total number of pencils you need to need to multiply 30 boxes $\times$ 25 pencils/box = 750, choice **B**.

Question 18 $25.95 + $39.50 + $65 + $19.99 = $150.44, choice **G**.

Question 19   Since pies cost $3 apiece, and the debate team made $228, $\frac{228}{3} = 76$ pies sold. **A**.

Question 20 $99 + $22 + $46 = $167, choice **G**.

Question 21   236 boxes $\times$ 12 candy bars/box = 2,832 candy bars, **A**.

Question 22   24 can be used as the common denominator. $\frac{1}{8} \times 3 = \frac{3}{24}$ and $\frac{6}{12} \times 2 = \frac{12}{24}$. $\frac{3}{24} + \frac{12}{24} = \frac{15}{24}$ which can be simplified to $\frac{5}{8}$, choice **F**.

Question 23 $768 - 34 - 65 - 193 = 476$ coins remaining, choice **C**.

Question 24 $9 - $2.48 - $0.97 - $1.08 = $4.47, choice **J**.

Question 25 $1,518 / 33 girls = $46 for each uniform, choice **B**.

Question 26 $385.57 + $208.25 + $146.92 = $740.74, choice **G**.

Question 27   375 students $\times$ 0.52 = 195 students, choice **C**.

Question 28 $1\frac{1}{8} \times 6 = 6\frac{6}{8}$ which can be simplified to $6\frac{3}{4}$. **F**

Question 29   48 boxes $\times$ 37 donuts per box = 1,776, choice **B**.

Question 30 $\frac{4,123}{7} = 589$ students, choice **H**.

LANGUAGE

This section tests your knowledge of grammar, most notably grammatical rules involving punctuation, capitalization, and usage. Common errors include uncapitalized proper nouns, misplaced or missing commas or quotation marks, and improper subject-verb agreement. While many students are naturally leery of grammar, bear in mind that this is a multiple-choice test, so you don't necessarily have to be perfect at grammar: You just need to be able to spot incorrect grammar when it occurs.

Each question in this section has four choices, and the fourth answer on the first 36 questions is always "Correct as is." If you look at a question and can find no error, reread the question carefully. If you still don't find an error, simply pick *Correct as is* and move on.

Questions 1–24: Capitalization, Punctuation, And Usage

These questions feature an underlined phrase that may or may not have errors in punctuation, capitalization, and usage. The goal is to identify the error, and then choose the answer choice that corrects the mistake.

Question 1   The past tense agreement is *finished*. **A.**

Question 2   No capitalization is needed. **G.**

Question 3   Although people often incorrectly shorten *would have* to *woulda*—which sounds a lot like *would of*—the correct form is *would have*. **C.**

Question 4   Correct as is. **J.**

Question 5   A colon is used before a list of items. **A.**

Question 6   *Brazilian* refers to food from Brazil; adjectives derived from names of countries are always capitalized. **F.**

Question 7   *Her and I* are being used as objects, so the correct form would be *her and me*. **A.**

Question 8   While *runners* is plural, the subject of the sentence is *One*, so the verb must be the singular is *trying*. **H.**

Question 9   There must be quotation marks at the end of the spoken text in order to close off the quote. **B.**

Question 10   The first use of the word *Governor, our governor* does not need to be capitalized. The second use is a title and therefore is capitalized. **G.**

Question 11   The underlined pronoun *our* refers to the *team*, so it should be changed to the third person pronoun *its*. **C.**

Question 12   *Its* is a contraction of *it is*, so there needs to be a apostrophe between the *t* and the *s*. **G.**

Question 13   A word that modifies a verb is called an adverb. Here, the correct adverb form is *quickly*. **A.**

Question 14   Since Michelle is speaking, her words must be set apart by balanced quotation marks. **H.**

Question 15   The phrase *a friendly version of the monster* modifies *dragon*, and needs to be placed within a set of commas. **C.**

Question 16   Parallel construction states that items in a list need to be similar parts of speech. Since the first items in this list are nouns, there is no need for the extra verb and pronoun *took her*. **F.**

Question 17   This question is similar to question 13, as the adjective *happy* needs to be changed to the adverb *happily*. **C.**

Question 18   Correct as is. **J.**

Question 19   *Doctor* is a title in the sentence, and needs to be capitalized. **A.**

Question 20   Semicolons separate two related sentences. **G.**

Question 21   There must be quotation marks at the end of the spoken text in order to close off the quote. **C.**

Question 22   The word *south* refers to a direction, not a specific region, in this sentence, so **F** is correct.

Question 23   The verb needs to be the plural *are going*. **C.**

Question 24   *Principal Moore* is a title, so the answer is **H.**

Question 25–36: Sentence Structure

These questions include boxed-in sentences that sometimes contain sentence structure errors, such as: sentence fragments, redundant words that need to be omitted, and incorrect punctuation. The goal is to identify the error and then choose the answer choice that fixes the problem.

Question 25 *Clapped and applauded* mean the same thing, so one must be eliminated. **B.**

Question 26 The two related sentences should be combined by replacing the period with a comma (the *And* then reverts to lower case). **G.**

Question 27 Sprinting and running mean the same thing. **A** is correct since it eliminates this redundancy.

Question 28 *But fair* is a sentence fragment. It should be combined with the first sentence. **H.**

Question 29 The phrase *Still in the refrigerator* modifies *lunch*, not *I*. **B** corrects this.

Question 30 **F** is the best solution for these contrasting statements.

Question 31 These two sentences need to be combined with either a conjunction or the changing of one into a phrase. **B** does the latter option.

Question 32 *Cried* and *sobbed* mean the same thing, so one must be eliminated. **G.**

Question 33 *Unwilling to surrender* is a phrase modifying *soldiers*, so it needs to be placed next to that noun. **A.**

Question 34 **H** separates this run–on sentence into grammatically correct sentences that convey the overall meaning correctly.

Question 35 *Swam through the water* is clearer and more correct. **A.**

Question 36 Andre is the one talking on the phone, while in the boxed sentence the cat is the one on the phone. **G.**

Question 37–48: Content and Organization

These questions are similar to Reading Comprehension questions, as students read a mini-passage and then answer questions about the text. These questions can therefore be approached in the same way as Reading Comprehension questions. There is also an occasional grammar problem that needs to be remedied.

Question 37 Since the last sentence is discussing the death of plants who do not receive all the ingredients needed to survive, **B** is the best choice to help qualify this statement.

Question 38 **F** is correct.

Question 39 **D** is the best choice, since the underlined sentence acts as a conclusion to the previous sentences.

Question 40 The paragraph is about Robert, but **H** is about the history of the blues.

Question 41 This paragraph is about Trevor, and **C** is discussing mountain foundations.

Question 42 As the first paragraph is totally complimentary, **G** is the best choice.

Question 43 **C** is best, as a semicolon is used to separate related sentences.

Question 44 **F** is the answer.

Question 45 **D** is off topic, as it talks about baseball in other countries, and not David, the baseball player.

Question 46 As the letter ends on a congratulatory tone, **F** continues this trend.

Question 47 **B** is the main idea.

Question 48 **J** is out of place, as the President's wife is not even mentioned in the paragraph.

SPELLING

Each of the thirty spelling questions has four answer choices. In the first three answer choices, one of the words in each sentence will be underlined. If you believe that this word is incorrectly spelled, that choice is the answer for that question. If you look over the first three choices and believe all the words are spelled correctly, then you must pick the fourth choice, which is always *No Mistake*.

Having a large vocabulary is the best key to doing well on the Spelling section. However, knowing how to add suffixes (such as the *-es* at the end of *suffixes*) is also an important skill, as many spelling errors occur when suffixes are incorrectly added.

Question 1   *Plane* is spelled *plain* as an adjective meaning *simple*. **C.**

Question 2   *Here* is spelled *hear* as the verb to *listen*. **H.**

Question 3   *Hole* is spelled *whole* as the adjective meaning *entire*. **B.**

Question 4   *Stares* is spelled *stairs* as the noun meaning *a flight of steps*. **G.**

Question 5   *Write* is spelled *right* as the adjective meaning *correct*. **A.**

Question 6   *Buy* is spelled *by* as the adjective meaning *next to*. **G.**

Question 7   *Attencion* is spelled *attention*. **C.**

Question 8   *Habbit* is spelled *habit*. **G.**

Question 9   *Errur* is spelled *error*. **A**

Question 10   *Billyun* is spelled *billion*. **G.**

Question 11   No mistake. **D.**

Question 12   *Chemistrey* is spelled *chemistry*. **F.**

Question 13   *Lekture* is spelled *lecture*. **C.**

Question 14   *Roomor* is spelled *rumor*. **F.**

Question 15   *Fortun* is spelled *fortune*. **C.**

Question 16   *Excellint* is spelled *excellent*. **G**.

Question 17   No mistake. **D**

Question 18   *Delaiys* is spelled *delays*. **G**.

Question 19   *Appllication* is spelled *application*. **B**.

Question 20   *Confuseing* is spelled *confusing*. **G**.

Question 21   *Exacttly* is spelled *exactly*. **B**.

Question 22   No mistake. **J**.

Question 23   *Remarkkable* is spelled *remarkable*. **C**.

Question 24   *Festtive* is spelled *festive*. **G**.

Question 25   *Collasal* is spelled *colossal*. **A**.

Question 26   *Reahearsal* is spelled *rehearsal*. **F**

Question 27   *Statistishan* is spelled *statistician*. **A**.

Question 28   *Desputed* is spelled *disputed*. **H**.

Question 29   *Congradulated* is spelled *congratulated*. **B**.

Question 30   *Appraisel* is spelled *appraisal*. **H**.

Strategy Recap

In this section, we review the test-taking strategies you read about in the **Answers and Explanations for Practice Test A.** We look at the material covered on the STAR exam and provide techniques designed to give you a better approach to each question type. Spend some time reviewing this summary before you begin the second exam.

Some general strategies you should keep in mind as you look at the different kinds of questions:

- Use *process of elimination*: Crossing out unlikely answers helps you to make educated guesses when you need to. Even eliminating one incorrect answer greatly increases your chances of getting the question right.

- Always answer every question, even if you have to guess. You don't get any points subtracted for guessing, but you do get a point if you are right!

- Don't get stuck on any one question. Do the questions you can first. You can always go back to the harder ones.

Remember, you can use the above strategies throughout the test. Now, let's look at each question type.

READING VOCABULARY
Synonyms

Over half the vocabulary questions are Synonym questions. The underlined words are usually nouns or verbs, but you will probably see a few adjectives or adverbs as well. As we've said before, while it's terrific to have a big vocabulary and be able to define all the words on the test exactly, you shouldn't worry if you can't. If you encounter a word you don't know, remember that you do not need to know the exact dictionary definition to get the question right. If you have a general idea of its definition, that should be enough to help you eliminate some answer choices and guess.

Remember, you can use the positive-negative technique to help you find the right answer. For example, let's say you don't exactly know what the word *laud* means, but you know that it means something positive. You can then go to the answer choices and weed out any negative-sounding words. A positive word won't have a negative synonym, and vice versa.

Multiple Meanings

A good strategy for Multiple Meaning questions is to figure out what part of speech the underlined word in the boxed sentence is. For example, if you know that the underlined word in the boxed sentence is a noun, you can eliminate any answer choices that use the underlined word as a verb or an adjective. This will usually leave you 1-3 answers to choose from.

Vocabulary-in-Context

In these questions, the goal is to see if you can figure out the meaning of the underlined word from the context of the entire sentence (which is why they are called Context questions). The key to understanding the underlined word is seeing how that specific word fits in with the sentence's meaning. A good way to do these questions is to read the sentence and look for clues to the definition of the underlined word. Next, come up with your own definition. Then go to the answer choices and find the word that is closest to the definition you came up with.

READING COMPREHENSION

The best way to do these questions is to read the passage to understand the main point. Next, head to the questions. However, you should *go back frequently* to the passage to make sure you have the correct answer. You may think it a waste of time to keep looking at the passage, but it isn't in the long run. The answers are in the passage, so why risk a wrong answer? Since you can always look at the passage, use it to find the best answer choice.

Some of the questions relate to two passages. To avoid errors, it's important to go back and look at the passages so you are sure you are working with the right information. Otherwise, you can approach these questions the way you would any Reading Comprehension questions.

MATHEMATICS—PROBLEM SOLVING

Here, you will find some word problems that have two or more steps. They usually require some reading, and may take 2-3 minutes to work on. (Others can be done faster). Remember that you don't get points subtracted for guessing on any part of the STAR tests. Therefore, you should always answer every question, even if you have to guess. Use process of elimination to get rid of unlikely answer choices whenever you can.

Number Sense and Numeration

Don't worry about big words like *numeration*. These questions test basic math concepts such as number lines, ordering numbers (from least to greatest or greatest to least), and expanded notation (for example, 6,000 and 30 and 4 = 6,034). Here, a good understanding of numbers and math principles helps a lot.

Number Systems and Number Theory

The questions in this category test a student's knowledge of such math concepts as prime numbers, scientific notation, as well as the basic facts underlying addition, subtraction, multiplication, and division. As in the previous category, a sound background in basic math principles is the best tool to succeed on these questions. If any of the phrases in the last two categories—such as scientific notation—are unfamiliar to you, make sure you learn about them before proceeding to the next test.

Algebra

These questions center around basic algebraic concepts such as solving linear equations, and finding the numeric value of variables. Be prepared to solve simple equations involving variables, such as $6f + 23 = 47$. Quite often, the value for the variable will be given in the question itself, so the best approach is to write out the linear equation with the variables first, and then substitute the numeric values given in the question.

Patterns and Relationships

As it name suggests, these questions test a student's ability to recognize and manipulate visual or mathematical patterns. For math patterns, the solution to the problem often involves addition or subtraction in some form.

Statistics and Probability

These questions usually involve a chart or graph. The best way to do well here is to learn about different kind of charts and graphs, such as pie charts, tally charts, line graphs, etcetera.

Geometry

These questions are mainly problems involving basic geometric shapes like squares, triangles, and circles. Sometimes there are a few questions testing your understanding of coordinates, symmetry, or rotation. Learn all the basic shapes, as well as the meaning of basic geometry terms like symmetry, and these problems should become quite simple.

Measurement

The largest category, many of these questions simply require a student to use a ruler and measure a figure correctly. Familiarize yourself with measuring objects using both metric and standard units. Other Measurement questions include counting change, comparing lengths, using the appropriate units (meters instead of gallons, for example), or reading a scientific instrument, such as a barometer, correctly.

Estimation

As the name suggests, Estimation problems require students to round off numbers properly to find the right estimate. To practice, take a very large number—the national debt, for instance—and spend time rounding off that figure to various units: the tens, hundreds, thousands, ten-thousands, hundred-thousands, and so on.

Problem Solving Strategies

This category covers a variety of different question types, but mostly these problems test whether or not you understand the steps needed you need to perform to answer the question.

MATHEMATICS—PROCEDURES

Many (about one-fourth) of the questions in this section are plain and simple arithmetical math problems. In this math section, as in the previous one, it is very important to write down all your work. Trying to do these questions in your head often leads to mistakes, and you will lose points on questions you really know how to do. So write down your work!

For this section, there are five possible answer choices, not the usual four. The fifth choice is always *NH*, which stands for *Not Here*. If you work a problem and then do not find the answer in the first four choices, rework the problem. If you get the same answer the second time, pick NH and move on to the next question.

Rounding

These questions are similar to the Estimation questions in the Math—Problem Solving section.

Computation-in-Context

These questions are mainly word problems. Read the text carefully, and then decide what math operation—addition, subtraction, multiplication, or division—needs to be performed to get the correct answer. Make sure you're comfortable with fractions, decimals and percentages.

LANGUAGE

This section tests your knowledge of grammar. While many students may not care too much for grammar tests, it's important to remember that this is a multiple-choice test: All you have to do is spot incorrect grammar when you see it. Most of the questions test grammatical rules involving punctuation, capitalization, and usage. Common errors include uncapitalized proper nouns, misplaced or missing commas or quotation marks, and improper subject-verb agreement.

Each question in this section has four choices, and the fourth answer on the first 36 questions is always "Correct as is." If you look at a question and can find no error, reread the question carefully. If you still don't find an error, simply pick *Correct as is* and move on.

Capitalization, Punctuation, And Usage

These questions have an underlined phrase that may or may not have errors in capitalization, punctuation, and usage. If you spot the error, try to think of the correct answer. For example, if you think a word needs to be capitalized and it isn't, imagine what the correct answer should look like. Then, look at the answer choices and pick the choice that connects with your mental image.

Sentence Structure

These questions feature boxed-in sentences that sometimes contain sentence structure errors, such as sentence fragments, words that need to be omitted, and incorrect punctuation. Again, look at the boxed-in sentence and try to anticipate what the correct answer should look like. For example, if you see a sentence fragment, decide yourself on what is the best way to eliminate the fragment. Then, look at the answer choices and find the choice that matches your idea.

Content and Organization

These questions are like Reading Comprehension questions; you will read a minipassage and then answer questions about the text. Therefore, you can use the same techniques as with Reading Comprehension questions. Remember to return to the passage often as you do the questions. There will also be an occasional grammar question on sentence structure or a grammatical problem to spot and correct.

SPELLING

Spelling questions have four answer choices, In the first three answer choices, one of the words in the sentence will be underlined. If you believe that any of these words are incorrectly spelled, that choice is the answer for that question. If you look over the first three choices and believe all the words are spelled correctly, then you must pick the fourth choice, which is always *No Mistake*.

As in the Language section, knowing how to spot an error, in this case, a mispelled word, can help you here even if you're not totally sure of the correct spelling. Knowing how to add suffixes (such as the *-es* at the end of *suffixes; blush, blushes*) is also an important skill, as many spelling errors occur when suffixes are incorrectly added. A large vocabulary is the best way to do well on this section, but process of elimination can also help a lot.

READY, SET, GO!

Now you've learned some skills that will help you on the second test, and on the STAR on test day. Feel free to go over them as often as you want before you go on to take the second test. You've also discovered what subjects you're good at, and what subjects you may need some more work in. Ask your parents, teacher, or friends for help in these areas. Just remember: These tests are just practice, and you are doing well by practicing and studying. Congratulations, and keep up the good work!

Quick Tips for Before and During the Test

Okay, you've taken Practice Test A and studied your test-taking strategies. You've focused on areas where your score was low and got help for those "Hot Spots." If you're still feeling a little nervous, here are more tips on how you can prepare for the STAR as test day approaches:

Just Before the Exam

- The best test takers do less and less as the test approaches. Taper off your study schedule and take it easy on yourself. Give yourself time off, especially the evening before the exam.

- Positive self-talk can be extremely liberating and invigorating, especially as the test looms closer. Tell yourself "I will do well" rather than "I hope things go well"; "I can" rather than "I cannot." Be aware of negative, self-defeating thoughts and images and immediately counter any you become aware of. Replace them with affirming statements that encourage your self-esteem and confidence.

- Get your act together sooner rather than later. Have everything (including choice of clothing) laid out in advance. You will gain great peace of mind if you know that all the little details—sharpened pencils, erasers, lucky shirt—are firmly in your control before the day of the test.

- Experience the test site a few days in advance. This is very helpful if you are especially anxious. If possible, find out what room you'll be assigned to, and try to sit there (by yourself) for a while. Better yet, bring some practice material and do at least a section or two, if not an entire practice test, in that room. In this situation, familiarity doesn't breed contempt, it creates comfort and confidence.

- Forego any practice on the day before the test. Keep the upcoming test out of your consciousness; go to a movie, take a pleasant hike, or just relax. And—of course—get plenty of rest the night before. Just don't go to bed too early. It's hard to fall asleep earlier than you're used to, and you don't want to lie there thinking about the test.

Handling Stress During the Test

The biggest stress monster will be the test itself. Fear not; there are methods of quelling your stress during the test.

- Keep moving forward instead of getting bogged down on a difficult question. You don't have to get everything right to achieve a fine score. The best test takers skip difficult material temporarily in search of the easier stuff. They mark the ones that require extra time and thought. This strategy buys time and builds confidence so you can handle the tough stuff later.

- Don't be thrown if other test takers seem to be working more furiously than you are. Continue to spend your time patiently thinking through your answers; it's going to lead to better results. Don't mistake the other people's sheer activity as signs of progress and higher scores.

- Keep breathing! Weak test takers tend to forget to breathe properly as the test proceeds. They start holding their breath without realizing it, or they breathe erratically or arrhythmically. Improper breathing interferes with clear thinking.

- Some quick isometrics during the test-especially if concentration is wandering or energy is waning-can help. Try this: Put your palms together and press intensely for a few seconds. Concentrate on the tension you feel through your palms, wrists, forearms, and up into your biceps and shoulders. Then, quickly release the pressure. Feel the difference as you let go. Focus on the warm relaxation that floods through the muscles. Now you're ready to return to the task.

With what you've just learned here, you're armed and ready to do battle with the test. This book and your studies will give you the practice you'll need to answer the questions. You also know how to deal with any excess tension that might come along, both when you're studying for and taking the exam. You've experienced everything you need to tame your test anxiety and stress. You're going to get a great score.

Practice Test B

Section 1: Reading Vocabulary

20 Minutes

30 Questions

Directions: *Make sure you have a watch to time yourself and a No. 2 pencil. When you are ready, start timing yourself, and spend 20 minutes answering the questions in this section. Mark your answers on the answer sheet provided. If you are finished before the time is up, check over your work.*

Reading Vocabulary

Synonyms

Directions

Select the word or set of words that mean the same as the underlined word.

Sample

To **congratulate** means to —

(A) discuss
● praise
(C) laugh
(D) listen

1 **Infinite** means —

(A) finished
(B) infirm
(C) eternal
(D) scary

2 **Scenic** means —

(F) theatrical
(G) beautiful
(H) visible
(J) important

3 An **objective** is a(n) —

(A) plan
(B) opinion
(C) picture
(D) goal

4 To **differ** means to —

(F) offer
(G) respect
(H) disagree
(J) enlarge

5 To **decrease** means to —

(A) increase
(B) lessen
(C) descend
(D) enlarge

6 To **examine** means to —

(F) pass over
(G) inquire
(H) study
(J) withstand

7 **Bilingual** means —

(A) speaking two languages
(B) playing two sports
(C) writing with both hands
(D) reading quickly

GO ON

8 <u>Hazard</u> is another word for —

    (F) reward
    (G) danger
    (H) invention
    (J) climate

9 To <u>postpone</u> something is to —

    (A) destroy it
    (B) forbid it
    (C) delay it
    (D) revise it

10 A <u>tyrant</u> is a —

    (F) servant
    (G) philosopher
    (H) politician
    (J) dictator

11 A <u>medal</u> is a kind of —

    (A) element
    (B) instrument
    (C) award
    (D) ceremony

12 <u>Primarily</u> means —

    (F) quickly
    (G) only
    (H) neatly
    (J) chiefly

13 <u>Mango</u> is a kind of —

    (A) fruit
    (B) dance
    (C) language
    (D) land

14 <u>Placid</u> means —

    (F) clean
    (G) healthy
    (H) calm
    (J) smart

15 To <u>laud</u> means to —

    (A) praise
    (B) listen
    (C) condemn
    (D) applaud

16 <u>Secure</u> means —

    (F) sacred
    (G) fastened
    (H) nervous
    (J) perfect

GO ON

Multiple Meanings

Directions

Read through the sentence in the box. Then select the answer in which the underlined word has the same meaning as the underlined word in the boxed sentence.

Sample

> **The group sounded best in a live concert.**

In which sentence does the word live mean the same thing as in the sentence above?

- Ⓐ The Johnsons live on Beal Street.
- Ⓑ The building repair exposed several live wires.
- ⬤ The TV network promised a live broadcast.
- Ⓓ The refugees live in hope of change.

17

> **It's a good idea to think about what you want to say, and to measure your words when you're angry.**

In which sentence does the word measure mean the same thing as in the sentence above?

- Ⓐ I could only count one measure in the music that had a different note in it.
- Ⓑ Chris took care to measure his words and never to say anything he didn't mean.
- Ⓒ I need to measure my windows so I can put up curtains.
- Ⓓ The tape measure is in the tool box.

18

> **Judge Marshall made a fair decision when she ruled against the plaintiff.**

In which sentence does the word fair mean the same thing as in the sentence above?

- Ⓕ She had lovely, fair skin.
- Ⓖ My uncle's apple butter won first prize in his county's fair.
- Ⓗ It didn't seem fair that nothing happened to the team that cheated.
- Ⓙ He had to be careful in the sun; he had such a fair complexion.

19

> **I had a lot to deal with between school, the hockey team, and my weekend job.**

In which sentence does the word deal mean the same thing as in the sentence above?

- Ⓐ You have to deal fast when you play gin rummy with grandma.
- Ⓑ There was a good deal of laughing when Tom told the joke.
- Ⓒ I got a great deal on the used car I bought last year.
- Ⓓ It was hard for him to deal with his brother going off to college.

GO ON

20

> The dancers swayed to the sound of the <u>beat</u>.

In which sentence does the word <u>beat</u> mean the same thing as in the sentence above?

- F The team found its opponents difficult to <u>beat</u>.
- G The owner was arrested because he <u>beat</u> his dog.
- H A steady <u>beat</u> is essential for any musical performer.
- J The priest <u>beat</u> the drum throughout the ceremony.

21

> The crowd was asked to <u>form</u> a straight line.

In which sentence does the word <u>form</u> mean the same thing as in the sentence above?

- A The test <u>form</u> was marked clearly with the letter C.
- B Stanley decided that wearing a hat was not good <u>form</u>.
- C The clerk filled out the <u>form</u> with his left hand.
- D To <u>form</u> a support group, the husbands met once a week.

22

> The new manager decided to <u>address</u> the issue in his speech.

In which sentence does the word <u>address</u> mean the same thing as in the sentence above?

- F The <u>address</u> of the designer's office was uptown.
- G The politician's <u>address</u> was long and tedious.
- H The facility was designed to <u>address</u> the needs of residents.
- J The homeless person was of no fixed <u>address</u>.

23

> My brother helped me <u>move</u> the couch into the family room.

In which sentence does the word <u>move</u> mean the same thing as in the sentence above?

- A The company newsletter announced a <u>move</u> downtown.
- B The movie promises to be so sad it will <u>move</u> you to tears.
- C This weekend, my family and I will <u>move</u> to a new town.
- D To repair it, I am going to <u>move</u> my car into the garage.

GO ON

Vocabulary-in-Context

Directions

In the sentence below, use the words surrounding the underlined word to figure out what it means.

Sample

Jeff reached the <u>summit</u> of the mountain, then began a long descent. <u>Summit</u> means —

- Ⓐ valley
- ● top
- Ⓒ clouds
- Ⓓ ridge

24 Mr. Lund reached the final peak of the mountain range, only to begin a <u>laborious</u> descent. <u>Laborious</u> means —

- Ⓕ speedy
- Ⓖ exciting
- Ⓗ spectacular
- Ⓙ difficult

25 The <u>latent</u> energy of the volcano was only released after years of inactivity. <u>Latent</u> means —

- Ⓐ stored
- Ⓑ powerful
- Ⓒ timid
- Ⓓ solar

26 The actor was <u>notorious</u> for making long, self-absorbed speeches during rehearsals. <u>Notorious</u> means —

- Ⓕ credited
- Ⓖ popular
- Ⓗ thanked
- Ⓙ infamous

27 Melissa was so <u>amiable</u> that she seemed to be friends with everyone. <u>Amiable</u> means —

- Ⓐ tired
- Ⓑ harsh
- Ⓒ friendly
- Ⓓ careful

28 Karen studied <u>thoroughly</u> for the exam, and therefore she had no problem answering any of the questions. <u>Thoroughly</u> means —

- Ⓕ quickly
- Ⓖ poorly
- Ⓗ slowly
- Ⓙ completely

29 As the sun began to <u>descend</u> in the evening sky, we turned on our bike lights so that cars could see us. <u>Descend</u> means —

- Ⓐ fall
- Ⓑ brighten
- Ⓒ darken
- Ⓓ enlarge

30 Since I had a tiny suitcase, I was limited to packing only <u>essential</u> things for vacation. <u>Essential</u> means —

- Ⓕ necessary
- Ⓖ tiniest
- Ⓗ flexible
- Ⓙ colorful

STOP ■

Answer Sheet

1 (A) (B) (C) (D)
2 (F) (G) (H) (J)
3 (A) (B) (C) (D)
4 (F) (G) (H) (J)
5 (A) (B) (C) (D)
6 (F) (G) (H) (J)
7 (A) (B) (C) (D)
8 (F) (G) (H) (J)
9 (A) (B) (C) (D)
10 (F) (G) (H) (J)
11 (A) (B) (C) (D)
12 (F) (G) (H) (J)
13 (A) (B) (C) (D)
14 (F) (G) (H) (J)
15 (A) (B) (C) (D)

16 (F) (G) (H) (J)
17 (A) (B) (C) (D)
18 (F) (G) (H) (J)
19 (A) (B) (C) (D)
20 (F) (G) (H) (J)
21 (A) (B) (C) (D)
22 (F) (G) (H) (J)
23 (A) (B) (C) (D)
24 (F) (G) (H) (J)
25 (A) (B) (C) (D)
26 (F) (G) (H) (J)
27 (A) (B) (C) (D)
28 (F) (G) (H) (J)
29 (A) (B) (C) (D)
30 (F) (G) (H) (J)

Section 2: Reading Comprehension

50 Minutes

54 Questions

Directions: *Make sure you have a watch to time yourself and a No. 2 pencil. When you are ready, start timing yourself, and spend 50 minutes answering the questions in this section. Mark your answers on the answer sheet provided. If you are finished before the time is up, check over your work.*

Reading Comprehension

Directions

Read the passage. Then answer each question that follows.

Sample

> When Margarita heard the weather report predict a severe thunderstorm within the half hour, she began to worry how her younger brother would get home from his friend's house. Certainly he couldn't walk all those blocks in the rain.

Margarita's brother was —

- Ⓐ doing his homework in his room
- ● at a friend's house
- Ⓒ playing in the backyard
- Ⓓ still at school

GO ON

Nature's Disguises

Animals have a variety of ways of protecting themselves from predators. Some animals adapt in shape and color to their environment. The tree frog, for example, blends perfectly into its surroundings. When it sits motionless, it is nearly impossible to distinguish it from a background of leaves.

Some animals change their coloring with the seasons. The caribou sheds its brown coat in winter, replacing it with a white fur. The stoat, a member of the weasel family, is known as the ermine in winter, because its brown fur changes to white. The chameleon is perhaps the most versatile of all animals that change their protective coloration. The chameleon changes its color in just a few minutes to whatever surface it happens to be lying on.

While most animals use their coloring as a way of hiding from predators, the skunk uses its *distinctive* white stripe as a way of standing out from its surroundings. Far from placing it in danger, the skunk's visibility actually protects it. By distinguishing itself from other animals, the skunk warns its predators to avoid its infamous stink.

1 **The author quotes the caribou and the chameleon as examples of animals that —**

- (A) change their color according to the season
- (B) protect themselves by changing color
- (C) sit still to blend with their surroundings
- (D) are able to change coloring within a few minutes

2 **The skunk is different from all the other animals described in the passage in that it —**

- (F) does not change its fur color in winter
- (G) protects itself by making itself visible
- (H) takes longer to change its fur coloration
- (J) can be smelled, but not easily seen

3 **As it is used in the third paragraph, the word *distinctive* most likely means —**

- (A) recognizable
- (B) expensive
- (C) fearsome
- (D) original

GO ON

This outline and the following **Works Cited** section are part of Monica's report on the brain. Use them to answer the questions that follow.

Lobes of the Cerebral Cortex

The brain is the most complex and mysterious organ in the human body. One thing we know is that the *cerebral cortex*—the thin outer covering of the brain—is incredibly important. These are the lobes, or sections, of the cerebral cortex:

The Frontal Lobe

Location: closest lobe to the face

Function: controls body movements

Damage Effects: paralysis; loss of control, particularly in fingers

The Parietal Lobe

Location: across the central fissure from the frontal lobe

Function: skin senses: touch, pressure, temperature

Damage Effects: inability to read and write

The Occipital Lobe

Location: near the back of the head

Function: vision

Damage Effects: loss of vision

The Temporal Lobe

Location: sides of the brain

Function: hearing

Damage Effects: loss of hearing

Works Cited

Amari, Hanna. "How the Brain Works." *Medical Digest* 8 April 1996: 22–28.

"Brains: The Different Parts." *The Life and Brain Journal* 1 November 1992: B9–B14.

Brent, Michael. *The Brain, Thoughts, and Dreams: How We Think.* New York: Arco, 1998.

Hingles, Kristen, ed. *The Medical Resource Book.* Boston: Claring, 1992.

Kamp, Joe. "Brain Waves." *Journal of Brain Research* 9 June 1990: 45–52.

"Living Brain Functions." *The Encyclopedia of Medical Arts.* 1984 ed.

New Mexico Center for Brain Research. *Three Decades of Brain Research.* Albuquerque, NM: National, 1999.

GO ON

4 Based on the information in the Works Cited section, which author wrote an article on brain waves?

- Ⓕ Michael Brent
- Ⓖ Hanna Amari
- Ⓗ Joe Kamp
- Ⓙ Kristen Hingles

5 How many lobes does the cerebral cortex have?

- Ⓐ 2
- Ⓑ 4
- Ⓒ 1
- Ⓓ billions

6 Based on the information in the Works Cited section, what did Kristen Hingles do?

- Ⓕ Illustrated a book that displayed the physical properties of the brain
- Ⓖ Authored a book that outlined the life and times of brain researchers
- Ⓗ Worked as an editor for a monthly journal on theories of brain functions
- Ⓙ Edited a medical resource book that covered general aspects of the brain

7 All of these should appear on the title page of Monica's report *except* —

- Ⓐ her first and last name
- Ⓑ the titles of all the articles she used
- Ⓒ the name of the class she is in
- Ⓓ the date the report was submitted

8 According to the outline, which of these is the cerebral cortex *not* responsible for?

- Ⓕ hearing
- Ⓖ vision
- Ⓗ speech
- Ⓙ skin senses

9 Where should Monica go if she wanted to know more about the recent history of brain research?

- Ⓐ *The Life and Brain Journal*
- Ⓑ *The Medical Resource Book*
- Ⓒ *Three Decades of Brain Research*
- Ⓓ *The Encyclopedia of Medical Arts*

10 Which of these questions is *least* relevant to the topic of the article?

- Ⓕ How large are the four lobes that make up the cerebral cortex?
- Ⓖ What has research told us about the human heart?
- Ⓗ What part of the brain is responsible for speech?
- Ⓙ Who are some of the most noted brain researchers?

11 Which of these CD-ROM software programs would be *most* useful in further researching this report?

- Ⓐ *Strange Facts about the Body*
- Ⓑ *The Medical Companion*
- Ⓒ *Multimedia Dreams*
- Ⓓ *Aspects of the Brain*

GO ON

The Trial

*This passage is adapted
from the writings of Mark Twain.*

I remember one of those sorrowful farces, in Virginia City, which we call a jury trial. A noted desperado killed Mr. B., a good citizen, in the most wanton and cold-blooded way. Of course the papers were full of it, and all men capable of reading read about it. And of course all men not dumb or idiotic talked about it. A jury list was made out, and Mr. T. L., a prominent banker and valued citizen, was questioned precisely as he would have been in any court in America.

"Have you heard of this homicide?"

"Yes."

"Have you formed or expressed opinions about it?"

"Yes."

"Have you read the newspaper accounts of it?"

"Yes."

"We don't want you."

A group of twelve men was inpaneled on a jury who swore they had neither heard, read, talked about, nor expressed an opinion concerning a murder which the very cattle in the corrals and the stones in the streets were aware of! It was a jury composed of two desperadoes, two low beer-house politicians, three barkeepers, two ranchmen who could not read, and three human donkeys! It actually came out afterwards that one of them thought stealing and arson were the same thing.

The verdict rendered by this jury was Not Guilty. What else could one expect?

The jury system puts a ban upon intelligence and honesty, and a premium on ignorance, stupidity and lying.

GO ON

12 **The main purpose of the passage is to—**

    Ⓕ illustrate that the jury system is in need of change

    Ⓖ describe the inhabitants of Virginia City

    Ⓗ entertain the reader with a tale of the frontier

    Ⓙ convince readers that the trial system is unfair

13 **Which of the following best describes the author's tone as indicated by the phrase, "What else could one expect?"**

    Ⓐ hope

    Ⓑ disgust

    Ⓒ suspicion

    Ⓓ astonishment

14 **Which of the following best summarizes the author's point in paragraph one?**

    Ⓕ Most intelligent people are aware of current events

    Ⓖ Few jury members are concerned about murders

    Ⓗ Stories about a murder affect the way people think

    Ⓙ Trial verdicts are generally what one would expect

15 **The author most likely quotes the jury committee's questions "Have you heard of this homicide?" in order to—**

    Ⓐ convey the internal state of a juror

    Ⓑ describe an exciting conversation

    Ⓒ indicate the foolishness of a system

    Ⓓ suggest the questions asked were unusual

GO ON

The Redfern Community Orchestra
Annual Holiday Concert
Center City High School
December 18
Tickets: $15, $10, & $5

For the past four years, the celebrated Redfern Community Orchestra has delighted audiences with its annual holiday concert. Conducted by David Lewis, the orchestra features community musicians of all levels and backgrounds. This season's concert will also feature guest soloists from the Los Angeles Academy of Music. On December 18, the Redfern Community Orchestra will offer a spectacular children's concert.

Children's Concert
4:30–6:00 P.M.

Program

1. Tchaikovsky's Symphony #4 (Excerpts)
2. Santa Claus is Coming to Town
3. Silent Night

4. Handel's Hallelujah Chorus
5. Hanukkah Medley
6. Jingle Bells

For tickets:

1. Visit the Redfern Community Orchestra Web site (www.redfernorch.org) and view the available seats.
2. Call Susan Farley, the Redfern Community Orchestra ticket representative, and tell her the seats for which you would like to purchase tickets.
3. Pick up your tickets one hour before the performance.

> The Redfern Community Orchestra needs your support. Please pledge whatever you can during our upcoming fund drive so we can continue to present wonderful, affordable concerts for the whole community.

The annual holiday concert was funded in part by a grant from the Los Angeles City Council.

GO ON

16 **Where will the concert be held?**

   (F)   The orchestra theatre
   (G)   Center City High School
   (H)   The town park
   (J)   Los Angeles City Council

17 **What is the third musical number on the program?**

   (A)   Hanukkah Medley
   (B)   Santa Claus is Coming to Town
   (C)   Jingle Bells
   (D)   Silent Night

18 **What is the purpose of the box towards the bottom of the flyer?**

   (F)   To ask for support
   (G)   To describe the orchestra
   (H)   To say how to get tickets
   (J)   To give a holiday message

19 **After you visit the orchestra Web site, what should you do to get tickets?**

   (A)   Pick them up at the box office
   (B)   Attend the concert
   (C)   Contact the orchestra's ticket representative
   (D)   The flyer does not say

20 **This flyer is most like —**

   (F)   a map
   (G)   a list of rules
   (H)   a catalogue of names
   (J)   an advertisement

21 **This flyer was written mainly to tell about —**

   (A)   the need for financial support
   (B)   a holiday concert
   (C)   the importance of music
   (D)   the Los Angeles Academy of Music

22 **Which of these is an opinion of the flyer?**

   (F)   …orchestra features community musicians…
   (G)   …concert was funded in part by a grant…
   (H)   …present wonderful, affordable concerts…
   (J)   …concert will also feature guest soloists…

23 **What kind of musicians play in the orchestra?**

   (A)   All levels and backgrounds
   (B)   Only professionals
   (C)   Only young children
   (D)   Particularly jazz players

GO ON

A Difficult Foe

The jellyfish is a simple but very interesting animal. Jellyfish have only two thin layers of living cells. Between these two layers, the jellyfish mostly consists of water. However, armed with stinging tentacles, the simple jellyfish is one of the few species that continues to *foil* attempts by human beings to control it.

Humans have tried a variety of methods to control jellyfish on beaches: nets, poisons, and even the introduction of jellyfish predators. All of these have failed. Furthermore, stinging jellyfish appear to thrive in waters polluted by sewage. This problem is so widespread that groups of stinging jellyfish have been known to block the pipes and cooling systems of power plants. For example, the mangrove jellyfish flourishes in polluted canals in the Florida Keys, making life difficult for the tourist industry in that area.

One type of jellyfish that has been the subject of many legends is the Portuguese Man of War. This jellyfish got its name because European explorers thought it looked like a Portuguese war ship. The Man of War is considered odd because it is not an individual but rather a colony of animals. The tentacles of the Man of War can reach over 150 feet. Despite its size, the Portuguese Man of War is nearly invisible to the unaided eye. The transparent animal appears pink, blue, or violet when viewed under special lights. Legends tell of a Man of War eating sailors alive. However, modern scientists say that this is impossible.

GO ON

24 According to the passage, what have humans *not* used to try to get rid of jellyfish?

- Ⓕ nets
- Ⓖ spears
- Ⓗ jellyfish predators
- Ⓙ poisons

25 According to the passage, the Man of War can —

- Ⓐ eat people alive
- Ⓑ turn invisible
- Ⓒ survive in polluted canals
- Ⓓ reach up to 150 feet

26 In the first paragraph, the word *foil* means —

- Ⓕ cover
- Ⓖ float
- Ⓗ sting
- Ⓙ stop

27 What is the main purpose of Paragraph 3?

- Ⓐ To describe a specific type of jellyfish
- Ⓑ To give general information about jellyfish
- Ⓒ To outline human attempts to kill jellyfish
- Ⓓ To predict the future of jellyfish

28 There is enough information in the passage to show that —

- Ⓕ humans will eventually overcome jellyfish
- Ⓖ jellyfish do not have any living cells in them
- Ⓗ the Man of War could eat a human being
- Ⓙ jellyfish are a strong species of animals

GO ON

Classified Ads

Diver

Scuba specialist needed for special assignments off the coast. Per job basis. Excellent salary. Knowledge of aquatic animals a plus. Responsibility a must. Call County Marine Center at 909-8976.

Doorman

People person. Great environment, paid vacation, benefits. Experience a must. Start $8.00/hr. Apply in person. Wed. 10–4. 4867 Amsterdam Ave.

Drummer

Jazz band needs great drummer for recording and touring. Great feel and solid time. No egos. Good opportunity for hard-working musician. Come to Context Studios, 6–8 pm, Sunday 9/18.

Dye Specialist

Fabric designer needs the right person to create the colors that make our product sell. Must have industry experience and a good attitude. Work well under pressure. Show us your stuff: Design Corp., 30 W. 9th St., 10009.

GO ON

29 **If you want to apply for the doorman position, you should —**

(A) call the building management
(B) send a résumé
(C) write a letter to say you're interested
(D) apply in person

30 **Which job requires you to send materials in the mail?**

(F) Dye Specialist
(G) Diver
(H) Drummer
(J) Doorman

31 **Which of these do you not need for the dye specialist job?**

(A) industry experience
(B) ability to work well under pressure
(C) flexible hours
(D) a good attitude

32 **Which job lists a starting salary?**

(F) Diver
(G) Dye Specialist
(H) Doorman
(J) Drummer

33 **If you want to apply for the dye specialist job, you should send —**

(A) a picture of yourself
(B) a letter of reference
(C) your school transcripts
(D) a sample of your dye work

GO ON

Document A

Science Experiment: How to Grow Bacteria

Ingredients

4 plastic containers
several slices of bread
set of measuring spoons
1 teaspoon salt

1 teaspoon sugar
warm water
magnifying glass

Procedures

1. Wash the containers with warm water.
2. Cut the bread into one-inch cubes.
3. Pour 2 tablespoons of water into 3 of the containers.
4. Add sugar to the water in one container and stir. Add salt to the water in another container and stir. Put bread in all 4 containers.
5. Check the containers daily.

Document B

Science Lab Safety Procedures

It is very important to keep safety in mind when working in the science lab. Otherwise, a serious accident could harm you and people around you. The most important rule of thumb is to use <u>common sense</u>. Don't do anything that you think might be dangerous. Ask your teacher for help if you are confused.

Working with Lab Materials

Always . . .
1. Carry test tubes with a pair of tongs.
2. Turn Bunson Burners off when you walk away from them.
3. Wash used beakers with soap and water.

Never ...
1. Touch chemicals with your fingers.
2. Take off your safety goggles when in the lab.
3. Take your eyes off the experiment you are doing.

A Quick Reminder

Lab safety is everbody's business!

GO ON

KAPLAN

34 Which of the following *best* describes the universal theme explored in these two selections?

- Ⓕ parasites
- Ⓖ recipes
- Ⓗ science
- Ⓙ life

35 What does Document B do that Document A does not?

- Ⓐ gives instructions
- Ⓑ adds a reminder
- Ⓒ involves bread
- Ⓓ describes an experiment

GO ON

Living Well in the Mountains

High in the Caucasus Mountains in southwestern Russia lie several small communities that share an interesting phenomenon. Many of these citizens live over one hundred years. Scientists have long wanted to know why these people live so long. A Russian scientist named Dr. Gogohian discovered a few important reasons.

First, Dr. Gogohian found that people in these communities are unusually active, regardless of age. They walk continuously on mountain roads in order to trade in the towns, and many of them chop wood and carry water to their homes. Another likely reason for these people's longevity is that they have a very good diet. Their diet includes many fruits and vegetables, dairy products, and nuts and grains. They eat only small quantities of meat, fat and salt. They don't consume any caffeinated drinks such as coffee or tea, and they don't eat sugar. They eat only very fresh, home-grown foods, and they don't eat big meals.

Several communities around the world have attempted to *mimic* the lifestyle of the Caucasus Mountain people. For example, in Tempe, Arizona, an organization has started to help people lead healthier lives. The program has not been in effect long enough to determine whether the participants will actually live longer or not. However, the people are definitely feeling better about themselves, and that is at least as important as living to be one hundred years old.

36 **Why did the author include the second paragraph?**

- Ⓕ To describe the landscape of the Caucasus Mountains
- Ⓖ To give the history of Dr. Gogohian
- Ⓗ To list the habits of the Caucasus Mountain people
- Ⓙ To outline a program in Tempe, Arizona

37 **Which of the following does *not* describe the lives of the Caucasus Mountain people?**

- Ⓐ They maintain a group exercise schedule
- Ⓑ They eat only small quantities of meat
- Ⓒ They do hard work everyday
- Ⓓ They walk a lot on mountain roads

GO ON

38 In this article, the word *mimic* means —

- F work
- G copy
- H exercise
- J carry

39 There is enough information in this passage to show that —

- A the Caucasus Mountain people are the happiest in the world
- B the people in Tempe, Arizona were not successful
- C cutting down on sugar will make you live to one hundred
- D Dr. Gogohian was very interested in the Caucasus Mountain people

40 Which of the following does the article *not* mention about the program in Tempe, Arizona?

- F The participants are feeling better about themselves
- G It guarantees that the participants will live longer
- H It is based on the lives of the Caucasus Mountain people
- J It is helping people change the way they live

41 The author's tone in this article is one of —

- A anger
- B interest
- C boredom
- D sadness

42 The boxes show some important aspects of the Caucasus Mountain people's diet.

vegetables

fruits

grains

Which of these belongs in the empty box?

- F dairy products
- G coffee
- H meat
- J sugar

43 You would most likely find this article in —

- A a travel brochure
- B a junior dictionary
- C a health magazine
- D a Russian history book

GO ON

Maureen's Umbrella

Maureen carried a small red umbrella in her right hand. She walked slowly through the park, gravel crunching under the soles of her rubber boots.

"I don't like the rain," Maureen said out loud. "Everyone's umbrella is prettier than mine."

In the distance Maureen saw her friend Kelly carrying a bright yellow umbrella with blue ducks on the border. Her other friend Monica had an umbrella made of clear plastic, and it was decorated with red and blue polka dots.

"I wish I had a nicer umbrella," Maureen sighed as she continued walking.

The park was roughly oval in shape, and it followed the contours of a lake which lay in the center. The rim of the lake was bordered by cherry trees, which were in full bloom.

Maureen paused under one of the cherry trees and *contemplated* her reflection in the water. A breeze brushed against her and as she looked at herself, she saw something remarkable—her plain umbrella was suddenly dotted with pink polka dots.

"What happened?" Maureen cried. She lowered her umbrella and examined it closely. The presence of tiny, pink polka dots had transformed the dull, red color of her umbrella to a brilliant scarlet. Maureen touched one of the polka dots, and she realized that it was nothing more than a thin, translucent cherry petal.

Maureen glanced at the cherry tree overhead, then ran to join her friends. "Look at my umbrella!" she cried.

GO ON

44 Maureen is unhappy because --

    Ⓕ   she thinks her friends have nicer umbrellas than she does

    Ⓖ   her boots hurt her feet

    Ⓗ   she is wet from the rain

    Ⓙ   she is late to school

45 The lake is located --

    Ⓐ   in the middle of the park

    Ⓑ   next to the school

    Ⓒ   far from the cherry trees

    Ⓓ   by her house

46 In paragraph 6, what does the word *contemplated* mean?

    Ⓕ   hoped

    Ⓖ   anticipated

    Ⓗ   expected

    Ⓙ   viewed

47 Why is Maureen happy at the end of the story?

    Ⓐ   Something nice and unexpected has occurred

    Ⓑ   Her friends are paying attention to her

    Ⓒ   It has stopped raining

    Ⓓ   She isn't lost anymore

48 What probably happens next in the story?

    Ⓕ   Maureen keeps how the umbrella got the dots a secret

    Ⓖ   The girls run to school because they are late

    Ⓗ   Maureen's friends admire the cherry petal umbrella

    Ⓙ   Maureen's friends tell her that her umbrella will be plain again soon

49 When does Maureen notice the changes of her umbrella?

    Ⓐ   When the petals began to fall off the umbrella

    Ⓑ   When she saw the umbrella's reflection in the lake

    Ⓒ   When she dropped it underneath the cherry tree

    Ⓓ   When Kelly and Monica told her

50 What would be another good title for this story?

    Ⓕ   *Maureen Hates the Rain*

    Ⓖ   *Walking to School*

    Ⓗ   *Rain and the Environment*

    Ⓙ   *The Magic Umbrella*

51 How did Maureen realize that the polka dots were made of petals?

    Ⓐ   They began to fall off

    Ⓑ   She touched one

    Ⓒ   Her friends told her

    Ⓓ   She had seen it happening

GO ON

The Classified

TV HIGHLIGHTS

MONDAY

7:00 P.M **Ch. 9** "The Lone Ranger." A biography of Charles Dutton, who spearheaded the grizzly bear rescue effort in Yellowrock Park.

8:00 P.M **Ch. 5** "Monday Night at the Box Office" presents *Another Brutal Thriller* (1996). Stars Emily Bleak in her breakthrough performance.

TUESDAY

6:00 P.M **Ch. 8** "The Book Files." Interview with Imogene Matthews, discussing her bestseller *Rainy Day Fun for Kids*.

7:00 P.M **Ch. 7** "Markie Goes to School." The ever-popular rabbit begins first grade, but not without a few mishaps. (Rerun.)

WEDNESDAY

8:00 P.M **Ch. 7** "Special Report: The Border Patrol." How Border Patrol agents cope with what they see as an impossible job.

9:00 P.M **Ch. 5** "Life Or Death." Season Finale. Dr. Abrahms and Nurse Jones's relationship takes a surprising turn. A terminally ill patient holds the ER hostage.

GO ON

52 If you watch Channel 5 on Monday at 8 P.M., you will see —

 Ⓕ a documentary on border patrol
 Ⓖ an interview with Imogene Matthews
 Ⓗ a movie with Emily Bleak
 Ⓙ a cartoon about a rabbit

53 Which show is a rerun?

 Ⓐ "Markie Goes to School"
 Ⓑ "The Book Files"
 Ⓒ "The Lone Ranger"
 Ⓓ "Life Or Death"

54 This listing is intended to appeal to —

 Ⓕ very young children
 Ⓖ lawyers
 Ⓗ college students
 Ⓙ the general public

STOP

Answer Sheet

1	A	B	C	D		28	F	G	H	J
2	F	G	H	J		29	A	B	C	D
3	A	B	C	D		30	F	G	H	J
4	F	G	H	J		31	A	B	C	D
5	A	B	C	D		32	F	G	H	J
6	F	G	H	J		33	A	B	C	D
7	A	B	C	D		34	F	G	H	J
8	F	G	H	J		35	A	B	C	D
9	A	B	C	D		36	F	G	H	J
10	F	G	H	J		37	A	B	C	D
11	A	B	C	D		38	F	G	H	J
12	F	G	H	J		39	A	B	C	D
13	A	B	C	D		40	F	G	H	J
14	F	G	H	J		41	A	B	C	D
15	A	B	C	D		42	F	G	H	J
16	F	G	H	J		43	A	B	C	D
17	A	B	C	D		44	F	G	H	J
18	F	G	H	J		45	A	B	C	D
19	A	B	C	D		46	F	G	H	J
20	F	G	H	J		47	A	B	C	D
21	A	B	C	D		48	F	G	H	J
22	F	G	H	J		49	A	B	C	D
23	A	B	C	D		50	F	G	H	J
24	F	G	H	J		51	A	B	C	D
25	A	B	C	D		52	F	G	H	J
26	F	G	H	J		53	A	B	C	D
27	A	B	C	D		54	F	G	H	J

Section 3: Math— Problem Solving

50 Minutes

52 Questions

Directions: *Make sure you have a watch to time yourself, a No. 2 pencil, and a ruler that has both metric and standard units. Use of a standard calculator is also permitted. When you are ready, start timing yourself, and spend 50 minutes answering the questions in this section. Mark your answers on the answer sheet provided. If you are finished before the time is up, check over your work.*

Mathematics— Problem Solving

Directions

Read each question and select the best answer. Then mark the space for the answer you selected.

Sample

The planet Mercury is about 5.8×10^7 km from the sun. What number is represented by 5.8×10^7?

- (A) 5,800
- (B) 580,000
- (C) 5,800,000
- ● 58,000,000

1 Put these fractions in order from least to greatest:

$\frac{7}{10}, \frac{3}{8}, \frac{2}{4}$

- (A) $\frac{3}{8}, \frac{2}{4}, \frac{7}{10}$
- (B) $\frac{3}{8}, \frac{7}{10}, \frac{2}{4}$
- (C) $\frac{2}{4}, \frac{3}{8}, \frac{7}{10}$
- (D) $\frac{2}{4}, \frac{7}{10}, \frac{3}{8}$

2 Rosa needs her thickest book to hold up a broken chair leg. She measures the four books on her desk. The first one she measures is $\frac{1}{4}$ inch thick. The other three are $\frac{7}{8}$ inch, $\frac{3}{10}$ inch and $\frac{5}{8}$ inch thick. How thick is her thickest book?

- (F) $\frac{3}{4}$ inch
- (G) $\frac{7}{8}$ inch
- (H) $\frac{3}{10}$ inch
- (J) $\frac{5}{8}$ inch

3 Put these in order from greatest to least:

$\frac{6}{12}, \frac{4}{6}, 1, \frac{3}{8}$

- (A) $1, \frac{6}{12}, \frac{4}{6}, \frac{3}{8}$
- (B) $\frac{3}{8}, \frac{6}{12}, \frac{4}{6}, 1$
- (C) $\frac{3}{8}, 1, \frac{4}{6}, \frac{6}{12}$
- (D) $1, \frac{4}{6}, \frac{6}{12}, \frac{3}{8}$

4 There are four pieces of styrofoam, all different lengths. The lengths of the pieces are: $\frac{3}{4}$ meter, $\frac{1}{2}$ meter, $\frac{2}{3}$ meter and $\frac{2}{6}$ meter. Which is the longest piece of styrofoam?

- (F) $\frac{3}{4}$ meter
- (G) $\frac{1}{2}$ meter
- (H) $\frac{2}{3}$ meter
- (J) $\frac{2}{6}$ meter

GO ON

5 Ethan measures how long four brands of batteries last for a school project. Brand A lasted $\frac{2}{3}$ of a day, Brand B lasted $\frac{3}{8}$ of a day, Brand C lasted $\frac{2}{4}$ of a day, and Brand D lasted all day. What is the least amount of time Ethan found a battery to last?

- (A) $\frac{2}{3}$ day
- (B) $\frac{3}{8}$ day
- (C) $\frac{2}{4}$ day
- (D) 1 day

6 Casey walks every day. She walked $\frac{2}{6}$ km on Monday, $\frac{7}{10}$ km on Tuesday, $\frac{9}{10}$ km on Wednesday and $\frac{1}{3}$ km on Thursday. Which day did she walk the farthest?

- (F) Monday
- (G) Tuesday
- (H) Wednesday
- (J) Thursday

7 Venus had a fever of 102.3 degrees. What is the value of the 3 in this number?

- (A) ones
- (B) tenths
- (C) hundredths
- (D) thousandths

8 The deepest point in the ocean is approximately 3.6×10^4 feet below sea level. How many feet are represented by that number?

- (F) 0.00036
- (G) 3,600
- (H) 36,000
- (J) 360,000

9 Each cube represents 0.01.

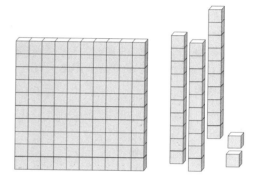

What decimal is pictured above?

- (A) 0.134
- (B) 1.34
- (C) 13.4
- (D) 134

10 In 1995, Los Angeles International Airport served approximately 5.4×10^7 passengers. What number is represented by 5.4×10^7?

- (F) 54,000
- (G) 540,000
- (H) 5,400,000
- (J) 54,000,000

GO ON

11 Dave sells refrigerators for $800. He will deliver a refrigerator for $2 for every mile traveled from the store. To determine total cost, he uses the equation

$c = 800 + 2d$

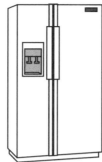

where c is total cost and d is number of miles traveled to the purchaser's house. The Newmans received their new refrigerator last week, as well as a bill for $900. How far do the Newmans live from Dave's store?

(A) 5 miles
(B) 50 miles
(C) 100 miles
(D) 2600 miles

12 Jenny has j muffins, while Billy has b muffins. y is the number of muffins that they have together. Write an equation to describe this situation.

(F) $y = b - j^2$
(G) $y = b^2 + j^3$
(H) $y = b + j - 2y$
(J) $y = b + j$

13 Georgia wants to buy an 18-inch necklace at the Gold Rope Jewelry Store. The cost, in dollars of a gold chain is calculated by using this expression:

$0.8g + 4$

where g is the number of inches of gold used and 4 is the price of a clasp. How much will Georgia have to pay for her 18-inch gold necklace?

(A) $10.40
(B) $13.80
(C) $16.00
(D) $18.40

14 For what value of x is $8x + 4 = 20$ true?

(F) 0
(G) 1
(H) 2
(J) 3

GO ON

15 The U.S. Rail Company prices its tickets using this formula:

$$c = 3m - 30$$

where *c* is the cost of the ticket and *m* is the number of miles of the trip.

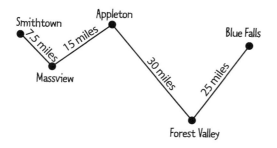

If Arthur's train trip cost him $60, which of the following cities did he travel between?

(A) Smithtown and Massview
(B) Massview and Appleton
(C) Appleton and Forest Valley
(D) Forest Valley and Blue Falls

16 The number machine below follows a rule that changes numbers into other numbers in the same way each time.

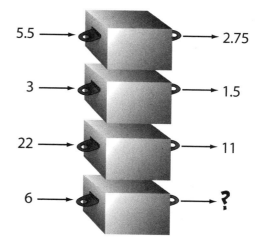

What number will 6 be changed into?

(F) 3
(G) 4
(H) 7
(J) 12

17 The table shows the temperature in degrees Celsius at various distances from a stove.

Distance	Temperature (°C)
2.5 feet	32°
5 feet	28°
7.5 feet	24°
10 feet	20°

If the pattern continues, at what distance will the temperature be 12°C?

(A) 5 feet
(B) 12.5 feet
(C) 15 feet
(D) 20 feet

GO ON

18 A computer program uses a formula to change numbers into other numbers.

The computer changed 2 into 4, 3 into 9, and 5 into 25.

What will the computer change the number 7 into?

- (F) 14
- (G) 21
- (H) 35
- (J) 49

Use the following information for questions 19 and 20. Tom planted several seeds. Two weeks later, he measured the heights of his plants. The results are as follows:

Plant	Height
1	2 in
2	5 in
3	1 in
4	2 in
5	3 in
6	6 in
7	2 in

19 What is the median of the plant heights?

- (A) 2 in
- (B) 3 in
- (C) 5 in
- (D) 6 in

20 Which plants have heights equal to the mode?

- (F) 1 and 5
- (G) 2, 5, and 6
- (H) 3 and 6
- (J) 1, 4, and 7

GO ON

Use the following information for questions 21 and 22 only.

Item	Price in 1957	Price in 1977	Price in 1997
Candy bar	$0.05	$0.25	$0.70
Movie ticket	$0.25	$4.00	$9.00
Novel	$0.75	$3.95	$12.00
Soda	$0.05	$0.45	$1.15
Fast food dinner	$1.65	$2.90	$5.35

21 If you went to a movie, bought a candy bar, and bought a soda in 1957, how much would you have spent?

- (A) $0.25
- (B) $0.35
- (C) $1.65
- (D) $4.70

22 If you bought a novel, a candy bar, and had dinner in a fast food restaurant in 1997, how much less would your great aunt have spent doing the same thing in 1957?

- (F) $10.30
- (G) $15.60
- (H) $18.05
- (J) $20.50

23 Eleanor Gray grows vegetables in her garden. One year, she harvested carrots, cabbage, corn, and cauliflower, as shown in the following graph.

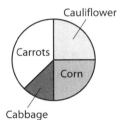

If Eleanor harvested 24 vegetables next year in exactly the same proportion, how many carrots should she expect to find?

- (A) 3
- (B) 9
- (C) 18
- (D) 24

24 Which of the following tally charts represents the data in the pie chart in question 23?

Carrots	ℍℍ ℍℍ ℍℍ III
Cabbage	ℍℍ I
Corn	ℍℍ ℍℍ II
Cauliflower	ℍℍ ℍℍ II

(F)

Carrots	ℍℍ ℍℍ II
Cabbage	ℍℍ ℍℍ II
Corn	ℍℍ ℍℍ ℍℍ
Cauliflower	ℍℍ III

(G)

Carrots	ℍℍ IIII
Cabbage	ℍℍ IIII
Corn	ℍℍ ℍℍ ℍℍ
Cauliflower	ℍℍ ℍℍ ℍℍ

(H)

Carrots	ℍℍ ℍℍ II
Cabbage	ℍℍ ℍℍ II
Corn	ℍℍ ℍℍ II
Cauliflower	ℍℍ ℍℍ II

(J)

GO ON

25 John and Yoko conducted an experiment for their math class, which is studying probability. They rolled a pair of dice 1,000 times and tabulated how many times they rolled a double, as well as how many times they rolled two different numbers. Their results are displayed in the pie chart below.

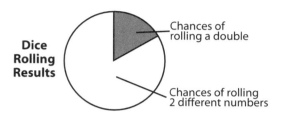

Dice Rolling Results

Chances of rolling a double

Chances of rolling 2 different numbers

If John and Yoko rolled a pair of dice 60,000 times, how many doubles would you expect them to roll?

Ⓐ 1,000
Ⓑ 10,000
Ⓒ 30,000
Ⓓ 60,000

26 Josie bought 2 shirts, a belt, and a pair of socks. How much did she spend?

Clothing	Cost
shirt	18.50
pants	21.00
belt	8.75
socks	3.25

Ⓕ $41.00
Ⓖ $49.00
Ⓗ $67.50
Ⓙ $85.00

27 If 40 hats were sold, how many of them would you expect to be black?

Distribution of Hat Colors Sold

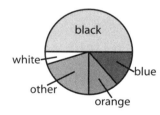

white
other
black
orange
blue

Total Hats Sold: 40

Ⓐ 5
Ⓑ 10
Ⓒ 20
Ⓓ 30

GO ON

28 How much fabric is needed to make this castle's flag? (Use $A = \frac{1}{2}bh$.)

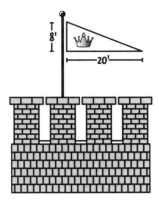

- Ⓕ 50 sq feet
- Ⓖ 80 sq feet
- Ⓗ 100 sq feet
- Ⓙ 160 sq feet

29 How much water can the aquarium in the figure hold? (Use $V = l \times w \times h$.)

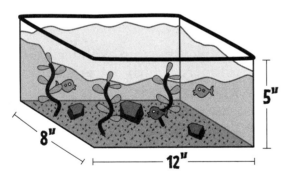

- Ⓐ 480 cu in
- Ⓑ 580 cu in
- Ⓒ 695 cu in
- Ⓓ 890 cu in

30 Which statement about this figure is true?

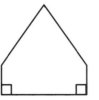

- Ⓕ There are no perpendicular lines.
- Ⓖ There are two acute angles.
- Ⓗ There are three right angles.
- Ⓙ There are two obtuse angles.

31

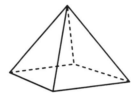

Susie is making a pyramid out of cardboard for an assignment on Ancient Egypt. Which of the following patterns can be folded into the pyramid above?

Ⓐ 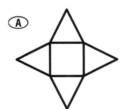   Ⓒ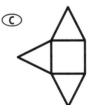

Ⓑ 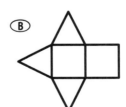   Ⓓ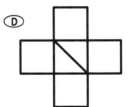

GO ON

32

If the tiles are blank on the other side, which tile is the same as the one above?

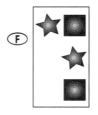

33 How many cubes are in this pile?

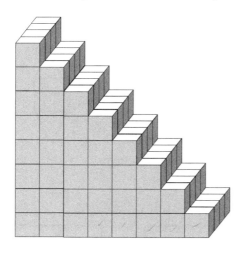

- (A) 32
- (B) 132
- (C) 144
- (D) 256

34

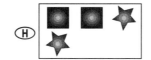

One triangle can be traded for two squares and two triangles can be traded for two stars. Which group of shapes below can be traded for three stars?

35

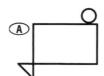

Timothy is making cylinders out of cardboard. Which pattern would fold into a cylinder?

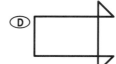

GO ON

KAPLAN

36 A spoke in the bicycle wheel in the figure is a good model for —

Spoke

- Ⓕ a diameter
- Ⓖ an arc
- Ⓗ a sector
- Ⓙ a radius

37 Use your centimeter ruler for this question. How long is the drawing of the carrot from the tip of the carrot to the end of the greens?

- Ⓐ 3 cm
- Ⓑ 8 cm
- Ⓒ 11 cm
- Ⓓ 14 cm

38 If the diving board is 7 feet long, how many feet long is the pool?

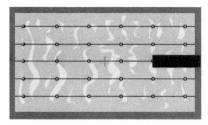

- Ⓕ 14
- Ⓖ 28
- Ⓗ 32
- Ⓙ 54

39 If the lamp is 4 feet tall, how many feet long is the sofa?

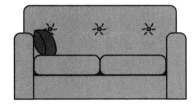

- Ⓐ 8
- Ⓑ 10
- Ⓒ 12
- Ⓓ 15

40 How many liters of water are in a kitchen sink that contains 5675 ml of water?

- Ⓕ 5.675
- Ⓖ 567.5
- Ⓗ 56750
- Ⓙ 5675000

GO ON

41 In the diagram below, 2 inches = 20 feet. If you lined up 3 trucks of this size, how long would they measure?

- Ⓐ 20 feet
- Ⓑ 35 feet
- Ⓒ 50 feet
- Ⓓ 60 feet

42 Scruffy the dog weighs $33\frac{7}{8}$ pounds. About how much does Scruffy weigh to the nearest pound?

- Ⓕ 32 pounds
- Ⓖ 33 pounds
- Ⓗ 34 pounds
- Ⓙ 40 pounds

43 Terence earns between $3 and $5 for each box of cookies he sells to raise money for his school's basketball team. If Terence's goal is to make $120 for the team, *about* how many boxes does he need to sell?

- Ⓐ 20 boxes
- Ⓑ 30 boxes
- Ⓒ 40 boxes
- Ⓓ 50 boxes

44 A city official recorded the number of car accidents in the city for each month of the year. His data for the first half of the year is shown in the table below.

Month	Number of Accidents
January	190
February	224
March	213
April	189
May	179
June	201

About how many car accidents were there during the first half of the year?

- Ⓕ 1,000
- Ⓖ 1,200
- Ⓗ 1,800
- Ⓙ 2,100

45 About how far is it from Alton to Danville along the road shown?

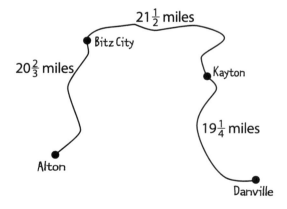

- Ⓐ 28 miles
- Ⓑ 38 miles
- Ⓒ $48\frac{7}{12}$ miles
- Ⓓ 60 miles

GO ON

46 A survey of 900 high school seniors found that 12% had a part time job. *About* how many of the students had a part time job?

- Ⓕ 12
- Ⓖ 90
- Ⓗ 240
- Ⓙ 888

47 Celeste measured the amount of water her guinea pig drank each day for a week, as shown in the chart below.

Day	Amount of Water (fl oz)
Monday	2.84
Tuesday	3.15
Wednesday	2.75
Thursday	3.21
Friday	3.01

About how much did the guinea pig drink over the whole week?

- Ⓐ 10 fl oz
- Ⓑ 15 fl oz
- Ⓒ 17.06 fl oz
- Ⓓ 23 fl oz

48 Henry did three subjects of homework. He started at 4:15 P.M. What else to you need to be told in order to find out how long Henry spent on his homework?

- Ⓕ What time he finished his homework
- Ⓖ What subjects he was studying
- Ⓗ How long it took him to eat dinner
- Ⓙ What time he went to soccer practice

49 Lucy and Ethel like to play sports on the weekend, but they like to play them only in a particular order. They never play tennis, baseball, or volleyball second. They never play baseball or volleyball first. They never play tennis or baseball last. What is the order in which they play sports?

- Ⓐ Baseball, tennis, hockey, volleyball
- Ⓑ Baseball, hockey, volleyball, tennis
- Ⓒ Tennis, hockey, baseball, volleyball
- Ⓓ Volleyball, hockey, tennis, baseball

GO ON

50 When Lucy gets home from school, she always follows the same routine. She does four things: eats her snack, talks on the phone, does her homework, and reads. She never does her homework last. She never eats her snack, does her homework, or reads third. She never reads or does her homework first. What is her afternoon routine?

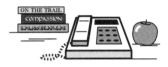

  (F) talks on the phone, eats her snack, reads, does her homework

  (G) eats her snack, does her homework, talks on the phone, reads

  (H) does her homework, reads, talks on the phone, eats her snack

  (J) reads, does her homework, eat her snack, talks on the phone

51 After Daisy woke up she got dressed, ate her breakfast, and brushed her teeth. She left her house to walk to school at 7:50 A.M. What would you need to know to find out how long it took her to get ready for school?

  (A) What she ate for breakfast

  (B) How long it takes her to walk to school

  (C) What time she woke up

  (D) What toothpaste she used

52 Jean-Marc insists on eating his dinner which consists of broccoli, potato, salad, and steak in a particular order. He never eats potato or salad first. He never eats broccoli, steak, or salad third. He will not eat broccoli or salad second. What is the order in which he eats his meal?

  (F) steak, salad, broccoli, potato

  (G) broccoli, potato, steak, salad

  (H) salad, potato, broccoli, steak

  (J) broccoli, steak, potato, salad

STOP

Answer Sheet

1	Ⓐ	Ⓑ	Ⓒ	Ⓓ
2	Ⓕ	Ⓖ	Ⓗ	Ⓙ
3	Ⓐ	Ⓑ	Ⓒ	Ⓓ
4	Ⓕ	Ⓖ	Ⓗ	Ⓙ
5	Ⓐ	Ⓑ	Ⓒ	Ⓓ
6	Ⓕ	Ⓖ	Ⓗ	Ⓙ
7	Ⓐ	Ⓑ	Ⓒ	Ⓓ
8	Ⓕ	Ⓖ	Ⓗ	Ⓙ
9	Ⓐ	Ⓑ	Ⓒ	Ⓓ
10	Ⓕ	Ⓖ	Ⓗ	Ⓙ
11	Ⓐ	Ⓑ	Ⓒ	Ⓓ
12	Ⓕ	Ⓖ	Ⓗ	Ⓙ
13	Ⓐ	Ⓑ	Ⓒ	Ⓓ
14	Ⓕ	Ⓖ	Ⓗ	Ⓙ
15	Ⓐ	Ⓑ	Ⓒ	Ⓓ
16	Ⓕ	Ⓖ	Ⓗ	Ⓙ
17	Ⓐ	Ⓑ	Ⓒ	Ⓓ
18	Ⓕ	Ⓖ	Ⓗ	Ⓙ
19	Ⓐ	Ⓑ	Ⓒ	Ⓓ
20	Ⓕ	Ⓖ	Ⓗ	Ⓙ
21	Ⓐ	Ⓑ	Ⓒ	Ⓓ
22	Ⓕ	Ⓖ	Ⓗ	Ⓙ
23	Ⓐ	Ⓑ	Ⓒ	Ⓓ
24	Ⓕ	Ⓖ	Ⓗ	Ⓙ
25	Ⓐ	Ⓑ	Ⓒ	Ⓓ
26	Ⓕ	Ⓖ	Ⓗ	Ⓙ
27	Ⓐ	Ⓑ	Ⓒ	Ⓓ
28	Ⓕ	Ⓖ	Ⓗ	Ⓙ
29	Ⓐ	Ⓑ	Ⓒ	Ⓓ
30	Ⓕ	Ⓖ	Ⓗ	Ⓙ
31	Ⓐ	Ⓑ	Ⓒ	Ⓓ
32	Ⓕ	Ⓖ	Ⓗ	Ⓙ
33	Ⓐ	Ⓑ	Ⓒ	Ⓓ
34	Ⓕ	Ⓖ	Ⓗ	Ⓙ
35	Ⓐ	Ⓑ	Ⓒ	Ⓓ
36	Ⓕ	Ⓖ	Ⓗ	Ⓙ
37	Ⓐ	Ⓑ	Ⓒ	Ⓓ
38	Ⓕ	Ⓖ	Ⓗ	Ⓙ
39	Ⓐ	Ⓑ	Ⓒ	Ⓓ
40	Ⓕ	Ⓖ	Ⓗ	Ⓙ
41	Ⓐ	Ⓑ	Ⓒ	Ⓓ
42	Ⓕ	Ⓖ	Ⓗ	Ⓙ
43	Ⓐ	Ⓑ	Ⓒ	Ⓓ
44	Ⓕ	Ⓖ	Ⓗ	Ⓙ
45	Ⓐ	Ⓑ	Ⓒ	Ⓓ
46	Ⓕ	Ⓖ	Ⓗ	Ⓙ
47	Ⓐ	Ⓑ	Ⓒ	Ⓓ
48	Ⓕ	Ⓖ	Ⓗ	Ⓙ
49	Ⓐ	Ⓑ	Ⓒ	Ⓓ
50	Ⓕ	Ⓖ	Ⓗ	Ⓙ
51	Ⓐ	Ⓑ	Ⓒ	Ⓓ
52	Ⓕ	Ⓖ	Ⓗ	Ⓙ

Section 4: Math—Procedures

30 Minutes

30 Questions

Directions: *Make sure you have a watch to time yourself, a No. 2 pencil, and a ruler that has both metric and standard units. When you are ready, start timing yourself, and spend 30 minutes answering the questions in this section. Mark your answers on the answer sheet provided. If you are finished before the time is up, check over your work.*

Mathematics— Procedures

Directions

Read each question and select the best answer. Then mark the space for the answer you have selected. If a right answer is *not here*, mark the space for NH.

Sample

Maria developed 24 pictures of her birthday party and 36 pictures of her sister's wedding. How many pictures did she develop all together?

- Ⓐ 50
- Ⓑ 59
- ⬤ 60
- Ⓓ 100
- Ⓔ NH

---

1   311
      × 93

- Ⓐ 404
- Ⓑ 2923
- Ⓒ 27,923
- Ⓓ 28,923
- Ⓔ NH

2 42)3,192

- Ⓕ 7
- Ⓖ 75
- Ⓗ 76
- Ⓙ 87
- Ⓚ NH

3   148
      × 909

- Ⓐ 14,312
- Ⓑ 134,522
- Ⓒ 134,532
- Ⓓ 1,432,942
- Ⓔ NH

4 1.6)0.64

- Ⓕ 0.004
- Ⓖ 0.04
- Ⓗ 0.4
- Ⓙ 4.0
- Ⓚ NH

5 0.9 × 591.28 =

- Ⓐ 532,152
- Ⓑ 53,215.2
- Ⓒ 5,321.52
- Ⓓ 532.152
- Ⓔ NH

6 $6\frac{3}{4}$
      $+ 3\frac{3}{4}$

- Ⓕ $9\frac{1}{2}$
- Ⓖ $10\frac{1}{4}$
- Ⓗ $10\frac{1}{2}$
- Ⓙ $11\frac{1}{4}$
- Ⓚ NH

GO ON

7   405
   × 289

    (A) 1,745
    (B) 10,745
    (C) 107,045
    (D) 117,045
    (E) NH

8   391
   × 54

    (F) 214
    (G) 2,014
    (H) 21,114
    (J) 22,114
    (K) NH

9 A farmer plants beets on 37% on his land. What is that percent rounded to the nearest fraction?

    (A) $\frac{1}{7}$

    (B) $\frac{1}{37}$

    (C) $\frac{1}{3}$

    (D) $\frac{2}{5}$

    (E) NH

10 The population of Kronhorstville is 6,574,836. What is this number rounded to the nearest hundred-thousands?

    (F) 7,000,000
    (G) 6,600,000
    (H) 6,570,000
    (J) 6,575,000
    (K) NH

11 The density of a certain asteroid is 4.54764 m/cm². What is this number rounded to the nearest hundredth?

    (A) 4.54760 m/cm^2
    (B) 4.5480 m/cm^2
    (C) 4.550 m/cm^2
    (D) 4.600 m/cm^2
    (E) NH

12 When rounded to the nearest whole number, $1\frac{19}{37}$ becomes

    (F) 0
    (G) 1
    (H) 2
    (J) 20
    (K) NH

13 Tripp loves Choc-O-Rific cookies.

If he eats five packages of these cookies this week, how many ounces of cookies does he eat?

    (A) $7\frac{1}{4}$

    (B) $6\frac{1}{4}$

    (C) $5\frac{1}{4}$

    (D) $4\frac{3}{4}$

    (E) NH

GO ON

14 Liz adopted 2 kittens from the pound. One weighed $4\frac{3}{8}$ pounds and the other weighed $3\frac{3}{4}$ pounds. How much did both kittens weigh together?

   Ⓕ $8\frac{3}{4}$ pounds

   Ⓖ $8\frac{1}{2}$ pounds

   Ⓗ $8\frac{1}{8}$ pounds

   Ⓙ $7\frac{1}{2}$ pounds

   Ⓚ NH

15 Matthew made $4\frac{1}{2}$ cups of macaroni and cheese. If one serving is $\frac{3}{4}$ cup, how many servings did Matthew make?

   Ⓐ 4

   Ⓑ $4\frac{1}{2}$

   Ⓒ 5

   Ⓓ 6

   Ⓔ NH

16 This summer, Middletown had only $2\frac{1}{6}$ inches of rainfall. Middletown usually gets $10\frac{7}{12}$ inches of rainfall in the summer. How many fewer inches of rainfall did Middletown get this summer than usual?

   Ⓕ $7\frac{6}{12}$ inches

   Ⓖ $7\frac{5}{6}$ inches

   Ⓗ 8 inches

   Ⓙ $8\frac{5}{12}$ inches

   Ⓚ NH

17 Daniel finished $\frac{3}{4}$ of his science project on Monday and $\frac{1}{6}$ of it on Tuesday. What fraction of his project had he finished by Tuesday?

   Ⓐ $\frac{4}{10}$

   Ⓑ $\frac{3}{10}$

   Ⓒ $\frac{4}{6}$

   Ⓓ $\frac{11}{12}$

   Ⓔ NH

GO ON

18 Christine and Colleen are twins. When they were born, Christine weighed $6\frac{3}{4}$ pounds and Colleen weighed $6\frac{7}{8}$ pounds. Together, how much did they weigh?

- Ⓕ $12\frac{3}{4}$
- Ⓖ $12\frac{5}{6}$
- Ⓗ $13\frac{5}{8}$
- Ⓙ $13\frac{1}{3}$
- Ⓚ NH

19 Keecia made $6\frac{2}{3}$ cups of lemonade. If one serving of lemonade is $\frac{2}{3}$ cup, how many servings did Keecia make?

- Ⓐ 5
- Ⓑ 6
- Ⓒ 9
- Ⓓ 10
- Ⓔ NH

20 A sports arena has 56 skyboxes. If 42 of them are owned by companies, what percent are company-owned?

- Ⓕ 14%
- Ⓖ 42%
- Ⓗ 56%
- Ⓙ 75%
- Ⓚ NH

21 A jacket that cost $54.50 is on sale at a 30% discount. If a man buys the jacket at the discount price, how much money will he save?

- Ⓐ $1.63
- Ⓑ $16.35
- Ⓒ $24.50
- Ⓓ $38.15
- Ⓔ NH

22 Josephine biked $5\frac{1}{4}$ miles on Wednesday, $2\frac{7}{8}$ miles on Thursday, and $6\frac{1}{4}$ miles on Friday. Combined, how many miles did she bike on these three days?

- Ⓕ $13\frac{3}{8}$
- Ⓖ $14\frac{3}{8}$
- Ⓗ $14\frac{5}{8}$
- Ⓙ $15\frac{3}{8}$
- Ⓚ NH

23 An infant weighs 8 pounds 11 ounces at birth. Two months later, the child had gained 3 pounds 7 ounces. How much did the baby weigh at 1 month?

- Ⓐ 11 pounds 2 ounces
- Ⓑ 11 pounds 8 ounces
- Ⓒ 12 pounds 6 ounces
- Ⓓ 12 pounds 8 ounces
- Ⓔ NH

GO ON

24 A fishing reel contains 420 feet of fishing line. If Monroe has used $240\frac{2}{3}$ feet of the line, what is the total number of feet remaining in the fishing reel?

- (F) $179\frac{1}{3}$ ft
- (G) $180\frac{1}{3}$ ft
- (H) $200\frac{2}{3}$ ft
- (J) $660\frac{2}{3}$
- (K) NH

25 Candace agreed with the car dealership to pay off her car loan of $2,212 in 28 monthly payments. If each payment is the same amount, how much will Candace pay each month?

- (A) $27.00
- (B) $78.50
- (C) $29.35
- (D) $92.15
- (E) NH

26 A recipe for a pot of gumbo calls for $\frac{4}{5}$ cup of okra to make 8 bowls of gumbo. How many cups of okra would be needed to make 10 pots of gumbo?

- (F) $\frac{4}{5}$ cups
- (G) 8 cups
- (H) 10 cups
- (J) $12\frac{1}{2}$ cups
- (K) NH

27 A piece of tape $2\frac{1}{3}$ feet long is needed to close up a packing crate. How many packing crates can be closed up from a roll of tape that is 56 feet long?

- (A) 18
- (B) $18\frac{1}{3}$
- (C) 24
- (D) $24\frac{1}{3}$
- (E) NH

GO ON

28 Blair works part-time during college as a bicycle courier. He uses his own bike and keeps track of the number of miles he bikes while delivering packages. One week he biked 17.3 miles on Monday, 12.8 miles on Tuesday, 4 miles on Wednesday, and 9.4 miles on Thursday. What was the total number of miles he recorded for that week?

- (F) 34.1 miles
- (G) 39.5 miles
- (H) 42 miles
- (J) 42.5 miles
- (K) NH

29 Linnea bought a new computer. She paid $2,643 for the computer, including $835 for a printer. What was the base price of the computer without the printer?

- (A) $1,808
- (B) $1,818
- (C) $2,559
- (D) $3,478
- (E) NH

30 A chef wants to make $\frac{2}{3}$ of a recipe for wild rice. The recipe calls for 16 pounds of wild rice. How many pounds will the chef need altogether?

- (F) 8 pounds
- (G) $10\frac{2}{3}$ pounds
- (H) $11\frac{1}{3}$ pounds
- (J) 24 pounds
- (K) NH

STOP

Answer Sheet

1	(A)	(B)	(C)	(D)	(E)
2	(F)	(G)	(H)	(J)	(K)
3	(A)	(B)	(C)	(D)	(E)
4	(F)	(G)	(H)	(J)	(K)
5	(A)	(B)	(C)	(D)	(E)
6	(F)	(G)	(H)	(J)	(K)
7	(A)	(B)	(C)	(D)	(E)
8	(F)	(G)	(H)	(J)	(K)
9	(A)	(B)	(C)	(D)	(E)
10	(F)	(G)	(H)	(J)	(K)
11	(A)	(B)	(C)	(D)	(E)
12	(F)	(G)	(H)	(J)	(K)
13	(A)	(B)	(C)	(D)	(E)
14	(F)	(G)	(H)	(J)	(K)
15	(A)	(B)	(C)	(D)	(E)
16	(F)	(G)	(H)	(J)	(K)
17	(A)	(B)	(C)	(D)	(E)
18	(F)	(G)	(H)	(J)	(K)
19	(A)	(B)	(C)	(D)	(E)
20	(F)	(G)	(H)	(J)	(K)
21	(A)	(B)	(C)	(D)	(E)
22	(F)	(G)	(H)	(J)	(K)
23	(A)	(B)	(C)	(D)	(E)
24	(F)	(G)	(H)	(J)	(K)
25	(A)	(B)	(C)	(D)	(E)
26	(F)	(G)	(H)	(J)	(K)
27	(A)	(B)	(C)	(D)	(E)
28	(F)	(G)	(H)	(J)	(K)
29	(A)	(B)	(C)	(D)	(E)
30	(F)	(G)	(H)	(J)	(K)

Section 5: Language

45 Minutes

48 Questions

Directions: *Make sure you have a watch to time yourself and a No. 2 pencil. When you are ready, start timing yourself, and spend 45 minutes answering the questions in this section. Mark your answers on the answer sheet provided. If you are finished before the time is up, check over your work.*

Language

Directions

Read each sentence, and focus on the underlined words. The sentence may contain an error in grammar, punctuation, or style. If you find a mistake, choose the answer that best corrects it. If you find no mistake, select *Correct as is*.

Sample

Their lack of fitness soon **become an issue** for the soccer team.

- ● became an issue
- Ⓑ become the issue
- Ⓒ become and issue
- Ⓓ Correct as is

1 When my cousin came to town, we went out to **eat chinese food**.

- Ⓐ ate chinese food
- Ⓑ ate Chinese food
- Ⓒ eat Chinese food
- Ⓓ Correct as is

2 Get the following things when you're at the **grocery store, eggs, bread, ice cream, and apples**.

- Ⓕ grocery store: eggs, bread, ice cream, and apples
- Ⓖ grocery store: eggs, bread, ice cream, and get apples.
- Ⓗ grocery store eggs, bread, ice cream, and apples.
- Ⓙ Correct as is

3 This is my morning **schedule of classes, French,** math, and gym.

- Ⓐ schedule of classes, french,
- Ⓑ schedule of classes French
- Ⓒ schedule of classes: French,
- Ⓓ Correct as is

4 The **titanic, a marvel of technology** when it was built, sank on its maiden voyage.

- Ⓕ Titanic, a marvel of Technology
- Ⓖ Titanic, a marvel of technology
- Ⓗ titanic a marvel of technology
- Ⓙ Correct as is

5 Of all the months of the **year February is** usually the coldest here.

- Ⓐ year, February are
- Ⓑ year february is
- Ⓒ year, February is
- Ⓓ Correct as is

6 One of the nation's enduring heroes **is General Grant, an** important figure of the Civil War.

- Ⓕ is general Grant, an
- Ⓖ is General Grant an
- Ⓗ are general Grant, an
- Ⓙ Correct as is

GO ON

KAPLAN

7 At the town meeting, <u>Mr. Haines the mayor, announced</u> he would not seek re-election.

- (A) Mr. Haines the Mayor announced
- (B) Mr. Haines, the mayor, announced
- (C) Mr. Haines the mayor announces,
- (D) Correct as is

8 The <u>companys' office was</u> located far from downtown.

- (F) company's office was
- (G) companys' office are
- (H) companys office were
- (J) Correct as is

9 Dan and Christopher made paper angels and snowflakes <u>to decorate their Christmas</u> tree.

- (A) to decorates their Christmas
- (B) to decorate their christmas
- (C) to decorated his Christmas
- (D) Correct as is

10 <u>Her and I like</u> to talk on the phone whenever we can.

- (F) Her and I likes
- (G) She and I like
- (H) She and me likes
- (J) Correct as is

11 Please <u>tell captain Vasquez</u> that funny story about your experience yesterday.

- (A) tell Captain Vasquez
- (B) tell captain vasquez
- (C) tells Captain Vasquez
- (D) Correct as is

12 The <u>caves opening</u> was large enough for a person to enter.

- (F) Caves opening
- (G) cave's opening
- (H) Caves' opening
- (J) Correct as is

13 Our <u>doctor, Doctor West was</u> able to tell me exactly why I was sick.

- (A) Doctor, Doctor West were
- (B) Doctor, Doctor West was
- (C) doctor, Doctor West, was
- (D) Correct as is

14 Give all the information to <u>officer Jenkins who</u> is standing over there.

- (F) officer Jenkins, who
- (G) Officer Jenkins, who
- (H) Officer Jenkins who
- (J) Correct as is

15 My mother's <u>High School is where the mayor</u> got his education.

- (A) high school is where the Mayor
- (B) high school is where the mayor
- (C) High School is where the Mayor
- (D) Correct as is

GO ON

16 Last night we ate dinner at <u>an italian restaurant</u>.

- ⒡ an Italian restaurant
- ⒢ an, Italian restaurant
- ⒣ a italian restaurant
- ⒥ Correct as is

17 Travel <u>East on Route 90</u> to get from Boston to Seattle.

- Ⓐ East on route 90
- Ⓑ east on route 90
- Ⓒ east on Route 90
- Ⓓ Correct as is

18 <u>Picasso, my favorite artist used</u> many different shapes in his paintings.

- ⒡ Picasso, my favorite Artist, used
- ⒢ Picasso my favorite artist used
- ⒣ Picasso, my favorite artist, used
- ⒥ Correct as is

19 Please give the information to <u>him and I so</u> we can use it later on.

- Ⓐ he and me so
- Ⓑ him and me so
- Ⓒ he and I. So
- Ⓓ Correct as is

20 Arturo and <u>him have thought</u> about starting their own business.

- ⒡ he has thought
- ⒢ he have thought
- ⒣ him has thought
- ⒥ Correct as is

21 I went to the library because <u>my book's were</u> overdue.

- Ⓐ my books were
- Ⓑ my book's was
- Ⓒ my books was
- Ⓓ Correct as is

22 Cary Grant was a classic <u>actor, his</u> movies are among the best ever made.

- ⒡ actor; his
- ⒢ actor his
- ⒣ actor; His
- ⒥ Correct as is

23 We had to go to the veterinarian because our <u>birds wing</u> was hurt.

- Ⓐ bird's wing was
- Ⓑ Birds' wing was
- Ⓒ birds wing were
- Ⓓ Correct as is

24 Karina <u>said, "That is a beautiful dress in the window.</u>

- ⒡ said, "That is a beautiful dress in the window."
- ⒢ said "That is a beautiful dress in the window."
- ⒣ said: "That is a beautiful dress in the window.
- ⒥ Correct as is

GO ON

KAPLAN

Directions

Read the sentence(s) in the box. If there is an error in sentence structure or logic, select the choice that best corrects it. If the sentence contains no mistake, select *Correct as is*.

Sample

> **You are the person. That everyone wants to be president.**

- Ⓐ You are the person. Which everyone want to be president.
- ● You are the person that everyone wants to be president.
- Ⓒ You are the person everyone wants. To be president.
- Ⓓ Correct as is

25

> **Professor Stevens, he said he wanted to see the fossil I had found.**

- Ⓐ The fossil I had found is what Professor Stevens said he wanted to see.
- Ⓑ Professor Stevens said he wanted to see the fossil I had found.
- Ⓒ He wanted to see the fossil I had found, said Professor Stevens.
- Ⓓ Correct as is

26

> **Blanche wanted candy, and she went to the store, and she bought some.**

- Ⓕ Blanche wanted candy, she went to the store, and she bought some.
- Ⓖ Blanche, wanting some candy. She went to the store and she bought some.
- Ⓗ Blanche wanted candy. She went to the store and bought some.
- Ⓙ Correct as is

27

> **In his later years, the singer performed his old hits in front of his adoring, worshipping fans.**

- Ⓐ In his later years, the singer performed his old hits, in front of his adoring fans, who worshipped him.
- Ⓑ The adoring fans whom heard the singer in his later years perform his old hits worshipped him.
- Ⓒ In his later years, the singer performed his old hits, in front of his adoring fans.
- Ⓓ Correct as is

GO ON

28

> Ken ran back to his house, he forgot the report that he wrote.

- Ⓕ   Ken, forgot the report that he wrote, he ran back to his house.
- Ⓖ   Back to his house, Ken ran and forgot the report that he wrote.
- Ⓗ   Ken ran back to his house. He forgot the report that he wrote.
- Ⓙ   Correct as is

29

> Lying on the grass, I found the bicycle where I had left it.

- Ⓐ   Lying on the grass, the bicycle I had left was where I found it.
- Ⓑ   I found the bicycle lying on the grass where I had left it.
- Ⓒ   I found the bicycle, where I had left it lying on the grass.
- Ⓓ   Correct as is

30

> Jenny was an artist, she always painted landscapes.

- Ⓕ   Jenny was an artist. She always painted landscapes.
- Ⓖ   Jenny was an artist who was always painting, landscapes.
- Ⓗ   Jenny was an artist, she always painted. They were landscapes.
- Ⓙ   Correct as is

31

> While Fred was busy with the cooking, his wife cleaned the living room.

- Ⓐ   While Fred was busy with the cooking. His wife cleaned the living room.
- Ⓑ   Fred was busy with the cooking, his wife cleaned the living room.
- Ⓒ   Fred was busy with the cooking his wife cleaned the living room.
- Ⓓ   Correct as is

32

> He was, of course, a brilliant pianist, that I loved to hear him play.

- Ⓕ   He was, of course, a brilliant pianist. I loved to hear him play.
- Ⓖ   He was, of course, a brilliant pianist I loved to hear him play.
- Ⓗ   He was, of course, a brilliant pianist, who I loved to hear play.
- Ⓙ   Correct as is

GO ON

33

> Playing at the local theatre, I wanted to see the movie.

   (A) It, the movie I wanted to see, was playing at the local theatre.

   (B) Playing at the local theatre were the movie that I wanted to see.

   (C) I wanted to see the movie that was playing at the local theatre.

   (D) Correct as is

34

> In the night sky the Big Dipper glittered brightly.

   (F) In the night sky glittering brightly was the Big Dipper.

   (G) Glittering brightly was the Big Dipper in the night sky.

   (H) The Big Dipper glittered brightly in the night sky.

   (J) Correct as is

35

> Because he was cautious and careful with money, Martin was able to save enough to buy a house.

   (A) Because he was careful with money, Martin was able to save enough to buy a house.

   (B) Because he was cautious, Martin, who was careful with money, was able to save enough to buy a house.

   (C) Martin, who was cautious and careful, he was able to save enough money to buy a house.

   (D) Correct as is

36

> In the store Betty found the dress; she had been looking at for months.

   (F) In the store Betty found the dress. Had been looking at for months.

   (G) In the store Betty found the dress she had been looking for it for months.

   (H) In the store Betty found the dress she had been looking at for months.

   (J) Correct as is

GO ON

Paragraph Questions

Directions

Read the paragraph in the box. Then read the following questions. Select the best answer to each question based on the information in the paragraph.

Sample

Paragraph 1

Koala bears look like cuddly animals. Through photographs, the button noses and furry ears of the Koala make them popular with children everywhere. But visitors to Australia are often surprised to find out what Koalas are really like. Koalas often hiss and spit at people when they come near.

Which is the *main* reason this paragraph was written?

- ● to tell you about Koalas
- Ⓑ to describe the animals of Australia
- Ⓒ to compare different animals
- Ⓓ to make sure visitors to Australia are happy

GO ON

Paragraph 1

A typical northern bog is a near-wetland ecosystem with soggy, poorly drained soil. The dominant plants in bogs are various species of sphagnum mosses, which absorb water like sponges. Bogs formed in shallow, hollow spaces of wilderness that were covered in glaciers 25,000 to 2.5 million years ago.

37 **Which of these would *not* belong in this paragraph?**

Ⓐ The glaciers scooped out long trenches in the earth's surface.

Ⓑ Mosses absorb water like sponges, and retain it for long periods of time.

Ⓒ Northern bogs are also known as sphagnum bogs.

Ⓓ Ansel Adams was one of the great wilderness photographers.

38 **Which of these would go *best* after the last sentence of this paragraph?**

Ⓕ Soggy, poorly drained soil is useless for farming.

Ⓖ As glacial ice melted, the hollow spaces in bogs were filled with water.

Ⓗ Sphagnum mosses are very pretty when dried.

Ⓙ As a result, pure new rainwater is the only source of oxygen for bogs.

39 **What is the *main* purpose of the paragraph?**

Ⓐ To explain what bogs are and how they came about

Ⓑ To describe the impact of glaciers

Ⓒ To compare sphagnum mosses to sponges

Ⓓ To list the various plants that live in bogs

GO ON

Paragraph 2

The circus is a fun place to visit. You can be a kid again! Don't be shy—pay your money, walk into the big tent, and watch the animals and the performers do their tricks. The huge elephants are as nimble as dancers. A man puts his head in a lion's mouth and then rides a tiger. The trapeze artists swing and somersault high above you. And best of all are the clowns, providing laughter for everyone.

40 **How can the first two sentences of this paragraph *best* be combined?**

- Ⓕ The circus, a fun place to visit, you can be a kid again!
- Ⓖ The circus is a fun place where you can be a kid again!
- Ⓗ The circus is a fun place to visit, you can be a kid again!
- Ⓙ A fun place to visit is the circus, and you can be a kid again!

41 **Which of these sentences would *not* belong in this paragraph?**

- Ⓐ You can eat cotton candy or hot dogs.
- Ⓑ There are jugglers riding horses.
- Ⓒ When I was a kid I wanted to be a big-league baseball player.
- Ⓓ The ringmaster keeps the action moving and tells you where to look.

Paragraph 3

Dear Robby,

I didn't think I'd like camp, <u>and</u> the first week has been pretty good. In the mornings we ride horses or hike the trails. Most afternoons we go blading or swim in the lake. We had a canoe race yesterday, and my cabin won! With all the different activities, it's easy to make friends. I'm already looking forward to coming back next year. Guess what—you'll be old enough to come then, too!

Be home soon,

Brian

42 **For which person would this letter *most* likely be written?**

- Ⓕ an older cousin
- Ⓖ a younger brother
- Ⓗ a father
- Ⓙ a teacher

43 **Which is the *best* substitute for the underlined word in the first sentence?**

- Ⓐ but
- Ⓑ since
- Ⓒ because
- Ⓓ if

GO ON

KAPLAN

Paragraph 4

Even though sushi recently became popular in the United States, it has been eaten in Japan for thousands of years. <u>Sushi is raw fish over white rice.</u> Sushi chefs in Japan practice their techniques over many years, and food is like an art to them. Although many Americans are nervous that they will get sick from raw fish, sushi chefs know that the fish is very fresh.

44 **Which of these is the *best* topic sentence for this paragraph?**

- (F) According to the chefs who make it, sushi is not as dangerous as people think.
- (G) Some people get sick from the food that they eat because it is not fresh.
- (H) Popular in Japan for thousands of years, sushi is an interesting mixture of raw fish and rice.
- (J) Sushi is very refreshing to eat on a warm summer day.

45 **What is the *best* way to begin the underlined sentence?**

- (A) However,
- (B) Basically,
- (C) Therefore,
- (D) Otherwise,

46 **Which of these would go *best* after the last sentence in this paragraph?**

- (F) Their knives are very clean.
- (G) Furthermore, a person can never get sick from sushi because the Japanese have been eating it for thousands of years.
- (H) Maybe the chefs should try freezing the fish to keep it fresh longer.
- (J) Surely other people will soon feel the same, and sushi will become even more popular.

47 **Which of these would *not* belong in this paragraph?**

- (A) American food consists of meat, grains, and vegetables.
- (B) The sushi chefs have great respect for their ingredients and are honored to make sushi.
- (C) The first person to make sushi found that the combination of fish and rice was delicious.
- (D) Sushi is very colorful food.

48 **What is the *main* purpose of this paragraph?**

- (F) To outline how chefs keep sushi fresh
- (G) To describe the art and history of sushi
- (H) To provide an opinion on the taste of sushi
- (J) To give an historical account of the first sushi makers

STOP

Answer Sheet

1	Ⓐ	Ⓑ	Ⓒ	Ⓓ
2	Ⓕ	Ⓖ	Ⓗ	Ⓙ
3	Ⓐ	Ⓑ	Ⓒ	Ⓓ
4	Ⓕ	Ⓖ	Ⓗ	Ⓙ
5	Ⓐ	Ⓑ	Ⓒ	Ⓓ
6	Ⓕ	Ⓖ	Ⓗ	Ⓙ
7	Ⓐ	Ⓑ	Ⓒ	Ⓓ
8	Ⓕ	Ⓖ	Ⓗ	Ⓙ
9	Ⓐ	Ⓑ	Ⓒ	Ⓓ
10	Ⓕ	Ⓖ	Ⓗ	Ⓙ
11	Ⓐ	Ⓑ	Ⓒ	Ⓓ
12	Ⓕ	Ⓖ	Ⓗ	Ⓙ
13	Ⓐ	Ⓑ	Ⓒ	Ⓓ
14	Ⓕ	Ⓖ	Ⓗ	Ⓙ
15	Ⓐ	Ⓑ	Ⓒ	Ⓓ
16	Ⓕ	Ⓖ	Ⓗ	Ⓙ
17	Ⓐ	Ⓑ	Ⓒ	Ⓓ
18	Ⓕ	Ⓖ	Ⓗ	Ⓙ
19	Ⓐ	Ⓑ	Ⓒ	Ⓓ
20	Ⓕ	Ⓖ	Ⓗ	Ⓙ
21	Ⓐ	Ⓑ	Ⓒ	Ⓓ
22	Ⓕ	Ⓖ	Ⓗ	Ⓙ
23	Ⓐ	Ⓑ	Ⓒ	Ⓓ
24	Ⓕ	Ⓖ	Ⓗ	Ⓙ

25	Ⓐ	Ⓑ	Ⓒ	Ⓓ
26	Ⓕ	Ⓖ	Ⓗ	Ⓙ
27	Ⓐ	Ⓑ	Ⓒ	Ⓓ
28	Ⓕ	Ⓖ	Ⓗ	Ⓙ
29	Ⓐ	Ⓑ	Ⓒ	Ⓓ
30	Ⓕ	Ⓖ	Ⓗ	Ⓙ
31	Ⓐ	Ⓑ	Ⓒ	Ⓓ
32	Ⓕ	Ⓖ	Ⓗ	Ⓙ
33	Ⓐ	Ⓑ	Ⓒ	Ⓓ
34	Ⓕ	Ⓖ	Ⓗ	Ⓙ
35	Ⓐ	Ⓑ	Ⓒ	Ⓓ
36	Ⓕ	Ⓖ	Ⓗ	Ⓙ
37	Ⓐ	Ⓑ	Ⓒ	Ⓓ
38	Ⓕ	Ⓖ	Ⓗ	Ⓙ
39	Ⓐ	Ⓑ	Ⓒ	Ⓓ
40	Ⓕ	Ⓖ	Ⓗ	Ⓙ
41	Ⓐ	Ⓑ	Ⓒ	Ⓓ
42	Ⓕ	Ⓖ	Ⓗ	Ⓙ
43	Ⓐ	Ⓑ	Ⓒ	Ⓓ
44	Ⓕ	Ⓖ	Ⓗ	Ⓙ
45	Ⓐ	Ⓑ	Ⓒ	Ⓓ
46	Ⓕ	Ⓖ	Ⓗ	Ⓙ
47	Ⓐ	Ⓑ	Ⓒ	Ⓓ
48	Ⓕ	Ⓖ	Ⓗ	Ⓙ

Section 6: Spelling

25 Minutes

30 Questions

Directions: *Make sure you have a watch to time yourself and a No. 2 pencil. When you are ready, start timing yourself, and spend 25 minutes answering the questions in this section. Mark your answers on the answer sheet provided. If you are finished before the time is up, check over your work.*

Spelling

Directions

If you see a word spelled incorrectly, mark it on your answer key. If no word is spelled incorrectly, select the "No mistake" answer choice.

Sample

- ● The wedding began <u>befour</u> noon.
- Ⓑ The depth of the water was hard to <u>measure</u>.
- Ⓒ My jacket was <u>stuck</u> in the door.
- Ⓓ No mistake

1
- Ⓐ She <u>bared</u> her soul to her best friend.
- Ⓑ He was a <u>vane</u> man, always looking in the mirror.
- Ⓒ I needed one more <u>board</u> to finish my ladder.
- Ⓓ No mistake

2
- Ⓕ I had to pay to repair the <u>break</u> on my car.
- Ⓖ The recipe called for two cups of <u>flour</u>.
- Ⓗ I have one <u>pair</u> of shoes that I have worn for years.
- Ⓙ No mistake

3
- Ⓐ I like <u>plain</u>, simple clothes.
- Ⓑ The brown <u>hare</u> ran across the road.
- Ⓒ I <u>poored</u> a glass of orange juice for breakfast.
- Ⓓ No mistake

4
- Ⓕ My arm was <u>sore</u> after I fell on it.
- Ⓖ Making bread requires you to <u>need</u> the dough.
- Ⓗ I <u>stared</u> at the picture until it became clear to me.
- Ⓙ No mistake

5
- Ⓐ Make sure you <u>close</u> the door behind you.
- Ⓑ The weather was sunny and <u>fare</u>.
- Ⓒ I want to <u>earn</u> money babysitting this weekend.
- Ⓓ No mistake

6
- Ⓕ This <u>callus</u> is small.
- Ⓖ I was <u>bored</u> during the movie.
- Ⓗ The <u>tension</u> was high.
- Ⓙ No mistake

GO ON

7
- Ⓐ That is not <u>allowed</u>.
- Ⓑ Hand me the <u>bynoculars</u>.
- Ⓒ It is a good <u>description</u>.
- Ⓓ No mistake

8
- Ⓕ They could not <u>repplicate</u> his work.
- Ⓖ Place the <u>shards</u> of glass over there.
- Ⓗ I want to be a <u>scientist</u>.
- Ⓙ No mistake

9
- Ⓐ Do not <u>interrupt</u> me.
- Ⓑ Watch the <u>horizon</u> for a storm.
- Ⓒ Is <u>calculus</u> tough?
- Ⓓ No mistake

10
- Ⓕ He was a good <u>influence</u> on the boy.
- Ⓖ The painting was <u>fascinating</u>.
- Ⓗ <u>Arkeology</u> is a neat subject.
- Ⓙ No mistake

11
- Ⓐ The <u>violin</u> was out of tune.
- Ⓑ The <u>deliberate</u> speaker talked slowly.
- Ⓒ Your ideas are not very <u>cohearent</u>.
- Ⓓ No mistake

12
- Ⓕ <u>Hazzardous</u> waste harms nature.
- Ⓖ Take these papers to an <u>accountant</u>.
- Ⓗ The tank <u>approached</u> slowly.
- Ⓙ No mistake

13
- Ⓐ An <u>elephant</u> has four knees.
- Ⓑ The outcome was <u>uncerten</u> when we left.
- Ⓒ The <u>choir</u> sang beautifully.
- Ⓓ No mistake

14
- Ⓕ Janet worked to save the <u>environment</u>.
- Ⓖ Put an <u>apostrophe</u> after that word.
- Ⓗ The building <u>annex</u> was secure.
- Ⓙ No mistake

GO ON

15 Ⓐ The laborers <u>toiled</u> in the factory.
Ⓑ What a <u>coincidence</u>.
Ⓒ The <u>flagun</u> of wine was spiced.
Ⓓ No mistake

16 Ⓕ There was <u>substanshal</u> evidence.
Ⓖ Write the <u>algebraic</u> formula on the wall.
Ⓗ <u>Recite</u> the school song.
Ⓙ No mistake

17 Ⓐ The dress was <u>fashionable</u>.
Ⓑ The <u>activation</u> program started.
Ⓒ Everyone said the Pledge of <u>Allegance</u>.
Ⓓ No mistake

18 Ⓕ His career was <u>ruined</u>.
Ⓖ The <u>laboratory</u> had been destroyed.
Ⓗ This is out of <u>sequence</u>.
Ⓙ No mistake

19 Ⓐ We climbed the <u>knoll</u>.
Ⓑ That name was a <u>seudonym</u> for Clemens.
Ⓒ The <u>temptation</u> was too great.
Ⓓ No mistake

20 Ⓕ We <u>aplauded</u> the singer.
Ⓖ Use the proper <u>technique</u>.
Ⓗ <u>Famine</u> is a serious problem.
Ⓙ No mistake

21 Ⓐ Will you respond to my <u>querys</u>?
Ⓑ The <u>politician</u> refused to answer.
Ⓒ The show ended <u>abruptly</u>.
Ⓓ No mistake

22 Ⓕ The <u>soot</u> is everywhere.
Ⓖ I told the <u>bureau</u> chief.
Ⓗ Woods <u>surrounded</u> the school.
Ⓙ No mistake

GO ON

23
(A) My <u>colleagues</u> are fools.
(B) It was a well-known <u>academy</u>.
(C) What a <u>prestigous</u> award.
(D) No mistake

24
(F) Clean the <u>chimney</u> more often.
(G) David could not <u>susstain</u> the effort.
(H) That was an <u>inept</u> dancer.
(J) No mistake

25
(A) Space is a <u>vacume</u>.
(B) The prisoner was <u>handcuffed</u>.
(C) There are <u>stains</u> on the wall.
(D) No mistake

26
(F) We bought a new <u>carpet</u>.
(G) Your <u>shelfs</u> are bare.
(H) Take the dishes to the <u>kitchen</u>.
(J) No mistake

27
(A) That old man is <u>ancient</u>.
(B) The <u>bronze</u> plate turned green.
(C) We were <u>convicted</u> quickly.
(D) No mistake

28
(F) The <u>villainous</u> man went to jail.
(G) The Greek <u>civilizasion</u> is quite old.
(H) The <u>burial</u> grounds were protected.
(J) No mistake

29
(A) Her <u>belated</u> Christmas gift arrived in March.
(B) The <u>antelope</u> runs fast.
(C) The <u>reasearch</u> company went broke.
(D) No mistake

30
(F) Keith is a <u>sophermore</u> in college.
(G) Collecting stamps is a <u>pastime</u>.
(H) <u>Botany</u> is her favorite subject.
(J) No mistake

STOP

Answer Sheet

1	Ⓐ	Ⓑ	Ⓒ	Ⓓ
2	Ⓕ	Ⓖ	Ⓗ	Ⓙ
3	Ⓐ	Ⓑ	Ⓒ	Ⓓ
4	Ⓕ	Ⓖ	Ⓗ	Ⓙ
5	Ⓐ	Ⓑ	Ⓒ	Ⓓ
6	Ⓕ	Ⓖ	Ⓗ	Ⓙ
7	Ⓐ	Ⓑ	Ⓒ	Ⓓ
8	Ⓕ	Ⓖ	Ⓗ	Ⓙ
9	Ⓐ	Ⓑ	Ⓒ	Ⓓ
10	Ⓕ	Ⓖ	Ⓗ	Ⓙ
11	Ⓐ	Ⓑ	Ⓒ	Ⓓ
12	Ⓕ	Ⓖ	Ⓗ	Ⓙ
13	Ⓐ	Ⓑ	Ⓒ	Ⓓ
14	Ⓕ	Ⓖ	Ⓗ	Ⓙ
15	Ⓐ	Ⓑ	Ⓒ	Ⓓ

16	Ⓕ	Ⓖ	Ⓗ	Ⓙ
17	Ⓐ	Ⓑ	Ⓒ	Ⓓ
18	Ⓕ	Ⓖ	Ⓗ	Ⓙ
19	Ⓐ	Ⓑ	Ⓒ	Ⓓ
20	Ⓕ	Ⓖ	Ⓗ	Ⓙ
21	Ⓐ	Ⓑ	Ⓒ	Ⓓ
22	Ⓕ	Ⓖ	Ⓗ	Ⓙ
23	Ⓐ	Ⓑ	Ⓒ	Ⓓ
24	Ⓕ	Ⓖ	Ⓗ	Ⓙ
25	Ⓐ	Ⓑ	Ⓒ	Ⓓ
26	Ⓕ	Ⓖ	Ⓗ	Ⓙ
27	Ⓐ	Ⓑ	Ⓒ	Ⓓ
28	Ⓕ	Ⓖ	Ⓗ	Ⓙ
29	Ⓐ	Ⓑ	Ⓒ	Ⓓ
30	Ⓕ	Ⓖ	Ⓗ	Ⓙ

PRACTICE TEST B

Answer Key

Reading Vocabulary

1 C
2 G
3 D
4 H
5 B
6 H
7 A
8 G
9 C
10 J
11 C
12 J
13 A
14 H
15 A
16 G
17 B
18 H
19 D
20 H
21 D
22 H
23 D
24 J
25 A
26 J
27 C
28 J
29 A
30 F

Reading Comprehension

1 B
2 G
3 A
4 H
5 B
6 J
7 B
8 H
9 C
10 G
11 D
12 F
13 B
14 F
15 C
16 G
17 D
18 F
19 C
20 J
21 B
22 H
23 A
24 G
25 D
26 J
27 A
28 J
29 D
30 F
31 C
32 H
33 D
34 H
35 B
36 H
37 A
38 G
39 D
40 G
41 B
42 F
43 C
44 F
45 A
46 J
47 A
48 H
49 B
50 J
51 B
52 H
53 A
54 J

Mathematics—Problem Solving

1	A	27	C
2	G	28	G
3	D	29	A
4	F	30	J
5	B	31	A
6	H	32	H
7	B	33	C
8	H	34	F
9	B	35	C
10	J	36	J
11	B	37	B
12	J	38	G
13	D	39	A
14	H	40	F
15	C	41	D
16	F	42	H
17	C	43	B
18	J	44	G
19	B	45	D
20	J	46	G
21	B	47	B
22	G	48	F
23	B	49	C
24	F	50	G
25	B	51	C
26	G	52	J

Mathematics—Procedures

1	D
2	H
3	C
4	H
5	D
6	H
7	D
8	H
9	D
10	G
11	C
12	H
13	B
14	H
15	D
16	J
17	D
18	H
19	D
20	J
21	B
22	G
23	E
24	F
25	E
26	K
27	C
28	K
29	A
30	G

Language

1	C	25	B
2	F	26	H
3	C	27	D
4	G	28	H
5	C	29	B
6	J	30	F
7	B	31	D
8	F	32	F
9	D	33	C
10	G	34	H
11	A	35	D
12	G	36	H
13	C	37	D
14	H	38	G
15	B	39	A
16	F	40	G
17	C	41	C
18	H	42	G
19	B	43	A
20	G	44	H
21	A	45	B
22	F	46	F
23	A	47	A
24	F	48	G

Spelling

1	B
2	F
3	C
4	G
5	B
6	F
7	B
8	F
9	D
10	H
11	C
12	F
13	B
14	J
15	C
16	F
17	C
18	J
19	B
20	F
21	A
22	J
23	C
24	G
25	A
26	G
27	D
28	G
29	C
30	F

How Did We Do? Grade Us.

Thank you for choosing a Kaplan book. Your comments and suggestions are very useful to us. Please answer the following questions to assist us in our continued development of high-quality resources to meet your needs.

The title of the Kaplan book I read was: _____

My name is: _____

My address is: _____

_____

My e-mail address is: _____

What overall grade would you give this book?   Ⓐ Ⓑ Ⓒ Ⓓ Ⓕ

How relevant was the information to your goals?   Ⓐ Ⓑ Ⓒ Ⓓ Ⓕ

How comprehensive was the information in this book?   Ⓐ Ⓑ Ⓒ Ⓓ Ⓕ

How accurate was the information in this book?   Ⓐ Ⓑ Ⓒ Ⓓ Ⓕ

How easy was the book to use?   Ⓐ Ⓑ Ⓒ Ⓓ Ⓕ

How appealing was the book's design?   Ⓐ Ⓑ Ⓒ Ⓓ Ⓕ

What were the book's strong points? _____

How could this book be improved? _____

Is there anything that we left out that you wanted to know more about?

Would you recommend this book to others?   ☐ YES   ☐ NO

Other comments: _____

_____

_____

Do we have permission to quote you?   ☐ YES   ☐ NO

Thank you for your help.
Please tear out this page and mail it to:

   Managing Editor
   Kaplan, Inc.
   888 Seventh Avenue
   New York, NY 10106

KAPLAN®

Thanks!

About KAPLAN

Kaplan, Inc. is one of the nation's leading providers of education and career services. Kaplan is a wholly owned subsidiary of The Washington Post Company.

KAPLAN TEST PREPARATION & ADMISSIONS

Kaplan's nationally recognized test prep courses cover more than 20 standardized tests, including secondary school, college and graduate school entrance exams, as well as foreign language and professional licensing exams. In addition, Kaplan offers a college admissions course, private tutoring, and a variety of free information and services for students applying to college and graduate programs. Kaplan also provides information and guidance on the financial aid process. Students can enroll in online test prep courses and admissions consulting services at www.kaptest.com.

Kaplan K12 Learning Services partners with schools, universities, and teachers to help students succeed, providing customized assessment, education, and professional development programs.

SCORE! EDUCATIONAL CENTERS

SCORE! after-school learning centers help K–10 students build confidence along with academic skills in a motivating, sports-oriented environment.

SCORE! Prep provides in-home, one-on-one tutoring for high school academic subjects and standardized tests.

eSCORE.com is the first educational services Web site to offer parents and kids newborn to age 18 personalized child development and educational resources online.

KAPLANCOLLEGE.COM

KaplanCollege.com, Kaplan's distance learning platform, offers an array of online educational programs for working professionals who want to advance their careers. Learners will find nearly 500 professional development, continuing education, certification, and degree courses and programs in Nursing, Education, Criminal Justice, Real Estate, Legal Professions, Law, Management, General Business, and Computing/Information Technology.

KAPLAN PUBLISHING

Kaplan Publishing produces retail books and software. Kaplan Books, published by Simon & Schuster, include titles in test preparation, admissions, education, career development, and life skills; Kaplan and *Newsweek* jointly publish guides on getting into college, finding the right career, and helping children succeed in school.

KAPLAN PROFESSIONAL

Kaplan Professional provides assessment, training, and certification services for corporate clients and individuals seeking to advance their careers. Member units include:

- Dearborn, a leading supplier of licensing training and continuing education for securities, real estate, and insurance professionals

- Perfect Access/CRN, which delivers software education and consultation for law firms and businesses

- Kaplan Professional Call Center Services, a total provider of services for the call center industry

- Self Test Software, a world leader in exam simulation software and preparation for technical certifications

- Schweser's Study Program/AIAF, which provides preparation services for the CFA examination

KAPLAN INTERNATIONAL PROGRAMS

Kaplan assists international students and professionals in the United States through a series of intensive English language and test preparation programs. These programs are offered at campus-based centers across the United States. Specialized services include housing, placement at top American universities, fellowship management, academic monitoring and reporting, and financial administration.

COMMUNITY OUTREACH

Kaplan provides educational career resources to thousands of financially disadvantaged students annually, working closely with educational institutions, not-for-profit groups, government agencies and grass roots organizations on a variety of national and local support programs. These programs help students and professionals from a variety of backgrounds achieve their educational and career goals.

BRASSRING

BrassRing Inc., the premier business-to-business hiring management and recruitment services company, offers employers a vertically integrated suite of online and offline solutions. BrassRing, created in September 1999, combined Kaplan Career Services, Terra-Starr, Crimson & Brown Associates, thepavement.com, and HireSystems. In March 2000, BrassRing acquired Career Service Inc./Westech. Kaplan is a shareholder in BrassRing, along with Tribune Company, Central Newspapers, and Accel Partners.

KAPLAN®

Want more information about our services, products, or the nearest Kaplan center?

Call our nationwide toll-free numbers:

1-800-KAP-TEST for information on our courses, private tutoring and admissions consulting

1-800-KAP-ITEM for information on our books and software

Connect with us in cyberspace:

On AOL, keyword:"Kaplan"
On the World Wide Web, go to:
1. www.kaplan.com
2. www.kaptest.com
3. www.eSCORE.com
4. www.dearborn.com
5. www.BrassRing.com
6. www.concordlawschool.com
7. www.KaplanCollege.com
Via e-mail: info@kaplan.com

Write to:

Kaplan, Inc.
888 Seventh Avenue
New York, NY 10106